A FLORENTINE PORTRAIT

A FLORENTINE PORTRAIT

Saint Philip Benizi (1233-1285)

by

D. B. WYNDHAM LEWIS

SHEED & WARD · NEW YORK

Manufactured in the United States of America

IN HONOREM
SEPTEM B.M.V. DOLORVM,
SERVIS EJVS PROV. ANGLIAE
SVMMA CVM OBSERVANTIA
OPVSCVLVM OBLATVM.

NOTE

The principal authorities and documents on which this sketch depends being acknowledged either in the text or in footnotes, a bibliography has been deemed unessential. The massive *Manuale* (1956) of Fra Alessio M. Rossi, O.S.M., has been consulted at every turn. Thanks are due to Fr. Gerard M. Corr, O.S.M., historian of the English Province, for very generous assistance and advice, to Miss Lucy Gooch for reducing a formidable manuscript to typescript with unflinching expertise, and to the St. Stephen's Secretariat for additional decipherings.

CONTENTS

A FLORENTINE PORTRAIT

I

THE CITY OF THE FLOWER

CHEWING in exile his bitter cud of memories, Dante has plenty to say in *The Divine Comedy* about his native Florence. Even amid the splendours and alleluias of Paradise he permits the ex-troubadour Falco to flame suddenly into denunciation of the City of the Flower, the devil's own weed, "planted by him who first turned his back upon his Creator":

> La tua città, che di colui è pianta
> che pria volse le spalle al suo Fattore ...

Fined and banished under pain of death in 1302, after the papalist party known as the "Blacks" seized power from the imperialist "Whites", Dante being at the time one of the six "White" priors or ruling councillors of Florence, the sombre poet neither forgave his city nor forgot. It is hardly surprising, therefore, that he never deigns to mention, in the *Commedia* or elsewhere, a very notable and saintly contemporary with whom he probably brushed shoulders in the streets more than once. Born thirty-two years after Fra Filippo Benizi, who became fifth General of the Servite Order and was canonised at length in 1671, Dante must, like any other Florentine of his day, have known the eminent friar at least by sight and repute for some time.

In Dante's boyhood, to begin with, Fra Filippo was a considerable public figure, deputed by a cardinal legate in

1279 to achieve the pacification of faction-torn Florence, and drawing immense acclaiming crowds to hear him in the Annunziata church, then nearing completion. The average Italian boy is some years more mature than the average Nordic boy of his age. Thirteenth-century Florence was a small, compact, walled city, about the size of Rye in Sussex, where everybody knew everyone else. The deductions seem plain and legitimate enough.

It is true that Fra Filippo Benizi was away from Florence for long periods during his years of activity. After 1254, when he threw up a successful medical practice and took the black serge habit of the Servite friars, he was for the most part either in retreat at Monte Senario, trudging the highroads of Europe to establish new Servite houses, or attending to the business of his order in Rome and other Italian cities. But his mission to the Florentines in 1276 was a notable event, following on his success in the same field at Bologna, and ended only when popular clamour threatened to force him into the vacant bishopric. Still more notable was his pacification-mission of 1279, when Fra Filippo was living for some time at the Annunziata priory in what is now the Via Cesare Battisti; Dante Alighieri being then aged fourteen and enslaved already— see the *Vita Nuova*—by Beatrice Portinari, a year his junior. In 1285, his last year on earth, Fra Filippo was again preaching at the Annunziata for a time. Dante was now twenty, not yet plunged into that period of wild living with Forese Donati and other boon-companions which he recalls with shame in the *Purgatorio*. It was two years since the famous second meeting with Beatrice in the street. Now the young wife of Simone dei Bardi, she had five more years to live. Quite possibly they both knew Fra Filippo, and he them.

One fact is certain. Whatever his pastimes and pre-occupations in the summer of 1286 Dante obviously knew about—and may even have participated in—the hubbub in the city following Fra Filippo Benizi's recent death at Todi, near Orvieto in adjacent Umbria, since the Florentines tried hard to bring their holy fellow-citizen's body home: once formally, armed with a brief extracted from Pope Honorius IV which was countered and foiled by a mass rising in Todi; and again a little later, and less formally, by an attempt at midnight theft, a *razzia* in the forthright medieval Italian manner. "Operation Foray" failed likewise. The alarm was given and the furious citizens of Todi rose again, recapturing Fra Filippo's coffin some distance beyond the gates and bearing it back to its tomb at San Marco in triumph. After two more attempts the Florentines gave up.

It is impossible to believe that a keenly perceptive young Florentine like Dante, and a rising poet to boot, took no interest in such picturesque nocturnal efforts to add to his city's treasures, or was unaware that by fleeing to the hills when offered the papal tiara some time before-hand Fra Filippo in his humility had disappointed his orgulous fellow-citizens most grievously. For this flight from the Keys, indeed, one or two of Dante's horde of commentators in half a dozen languages have actually included St. Philip Benizi in the short list of candidates for that place in the vestibule of Hell allotted by the ruthless poet to "him who made the great refusal", *il gran rifiuto*. By the majority of Dantophiles this judgment is supposed to apply, quite unfairly, to the frail old saintly monk Pietro di Murrone, Pope Celestine V, who was crowned against his will, reigned for five months in 1294, resigned, returned to his cell to die, and was later canonised at Avignon. Those authorities who elect St. Philip to St. Celestine's place in the *Inferno* are a small and relatively uninspired minority of the Italian wing, it might be added. The non-Italian list has at one time or another included Esau, Pontius Pilate, and St. Peter himself.[1]

One finds it again hard to believe that a Florentine of such civic consciousness and standing as Dante Alighieri became in ripe years never set foot in the great new Servite church of the Santissima Annunziata which replaced the oratory chapel of Cafaggio. Building began towards the end of 1264 and the church was completed long before the poet's banishment. Though it was not the basilica we know to-day, reconstructed by Michelozzo and adorned by Andrea del Sarto and others in later centuries, the Annunziata was even in Dante's time one of the jewels of Florence. The order to which it belonged, and of which Fra Filippo Benizi became General in 1267, had incidentally created some buzz in Florence in 1244, when malevolent tongues accused these new-fangled friars of propagating a form of the Manichean heresy known as the Paterine, and an inquisitor had to be sent to examine them. They cleared themselves with ease of a fantastic charge, but small-town gossip would long remember it.

All these things considered, one may venture to guess that Dante's omission of all mention of Fra Filippo might be deliberate. The role of the city of Florence in the *Divina Commedia* is chiefly to swell the population of Hell; a quite arbitrary whimsy on Dante's part, as need hardly be remarked, and a fine prideful usurpation of the judicial powers of his Creator. So it may be that any contemporary goodness flourishing in Florence had to be ignored

[1] Masseron (Alexandre), *Les Énigmes de la Divine Comédie.* Paris, 1921.

by Dante for purely artistic reasons; it spoiled what Whistler would call the "arrangement in black and crimson". Yet could Dante have produced a better stick with which to beat a few of the notable Florentines he consigns to eternal perdition—Argenti, Farinata, Cavalcanti, Ciacco, and a dozen more—than the shining sanctity of Philip Benizi?

For some years, then, Dante Alighieri and St. Philip walked the streets of the ever-enchanting City of the Flower, *Fiorenza*, at the same period, breathing that crystalline air, *aer luminosa*, which even to-day, notwithstanding the fumes of Progress, is like the breath of the first exquisite morning of Creation, whether Florentine skies are blue, or grey, or sending down lavish rain. During the first half of St. Philip's life Florence was not the architectural treasure-city it was becoming some years before his death. There was as yet no Duomo, with the noble Bruneschelli dome and the slender, soaring Giotto campanile; a church called Santa Reparata stood on the site. The Baptistery, not yet Dante's *bel San Giovanni*, was a smaller octagonal church, with a façade of green and white marble. There was no towering Palazzo della Signoria, with its loggia, in the main piazza, no Santa Croce or Santa Maria Novella, no Bargello, no Annunziata and Hospice of the Innocents with the lovely Della Robbia frieze. The Ponte Vecchio ("Old Bridge") over the smooth-sliding emerald waters of the Arno was still new and was called the Ponte Rubaconte. It had been the scene, on the morning of Easter Sunday 1215, of one of the first really spectacular assassinations in medieval Florentine annals, when gay young Buondelmonte dei Buondelmonti in his jewelled white finery was pulled off his horse by some of the Amidei family, whom he had publicly insulted, stabbed full of holes, and paraded dying through the streets.

We may picture the city in most of St. Philip's time as full of small, strongly-fortified palaces, each with its tower, built square for the Guelfs (or "Blacks"), and round for the Ghibellines (or "Whites"); the Guelfs being democratico-nationalist partisans, all over Italy, of the temporal power of the Holy See in its feudal territories, the Ghibellines demonstrating, equally all over Italy, for the nobility and the rule of the Holy Roman Emperor, who until 1250 was that fat, small, bald, cultured, violent, thrice-excommunicate ally of the Infidel crowned as Frederic II of Hohenstaufen and known as *Stupor Mundi*. Over and above recurring clashes in the streets at Florence between these two main factions of fierce impulsive men, there was frequent sword- and dagger-play in standing clan-feuds on the Highland pattern, also fought out publicly. The bright fantastic dress of the citizens, gowned, cloaked or armoured, may be seen in any illuminated manuscript of the period. These Florentines were, including the women, addicted to good and evil no less and no more than any other human beings of any age, with Tuscan vitality in each case superadded; and the worst ruffians and the most brazen mopsies of Florence, as we shall perceive, were capable of turning suddenly and permanently penitent, even saintly; a trick of which the modern world seems to some extent to have lost the secret. Outside the city walls, the same silvery ring of olive-groves and green-black cypresses on their low hills as we see them to-day, bathed in the same clear light. The city smells have changed. The Florentines of 1959 are poisoned chiefly by exhaust-fumes like the rest of us. In

the thirteenth century the wind in a certain direction bore
the fragrance of the main Florentine sewer, which was
open to the sky and, however formidable to the nose, perfectly harmless, as the best modern sanitation authorities
agree.

To-day in the immense Santissima Annunziata basilica
on any feast of Our Lady it is possible to go back seven
centuries very easily. Crowds of the same dimensions
throng the beautiful airy church with its crimson festal
hangings and crystal chandeliers, its myriad waxlights, its
marble and mosaic and goldwork. Under the Mass-
vestments of the celebrants is the same Servite habit of
frugal black serge. The same venerated picture painted
by Bartolommeo, save for Our Lady's features—supplied,
says local legend, by an angel and mysteriously uncopiable
by human brush—is unveiled for the same long, slow-
shuffling queues. The striking clay bust and deathmask of
St. Philip preserved at the priory, and the frescoes of his
life by Andrea del Sarto in the entrance cloister, bring his
presence very near. And if, after Mass, the visitor wisely
elects to avoid the smart restaurants and to eat and drink
with the native in some noisy, smoky *trattoria* well off the
tourist-track and far from the Anglo-Saxon maiden
ladies, he will be surprised to perceive how little the traditional Florentine, laughing, sharp-tongued and mocking,
must change down the ages. "Very smart jokers and
japers", says the celebrated Fra Salimbene di Adamo of
his fellow-citizens of the thirteenth century—*Florentini,
qui trufatores maximi sunt*. Observers acquainted with the
local argot say that the same quick, vivid, shapely phrases,
spiced with a dash of malice and sardonic Rabelaisian
gaiety, are still the Florentine norm. There are, and were,
exceptions. Fra Salimbene, an excellent friar though

scarcely a saint, is himself a jocular character in the medieval Italian-Franciscan tradition, counting M. Étienne Gilson among his warmest friends to-day. In St. Philip Benizi's deathmask, which bequeathes us a typical Florentine face, distantly recalling Dante's, less oppressively intense than Savonarola's, we perceive that mingling of gravity with sweetness which may be viewed also in what seems to be the only authentic portrait of St. Francis of Assisi, the one at Subiaco. During the period in which St. Philip practised as a rising young doctor of medicine, his bedside manner must have been perfection.

Being one of the relatively few medical saints in the Calendar, following in the wake of St. Luke and SS. Cosmas and Damian, he was qualified all his life to heal soul and body simultaneously. He certainly sacrificed much. It is not difficult to comprehend the outspoken dismay with which his father, a prosperous merchant—a parallel with St. Francis' case is visible—is said to have welcomed his only son's decision to throw up a lucrative professional career for the life of a mendicant friar, and in a new and as yet officially-unrecognised order at that. The attitude of Messer Giacomo Benizi, if authentic, affords a useful corrective to the tendency to regard the Ages of Faith as steeped everywhere in transcendental piety, which they were certainly not. Without doing Messer Giacomo the injustice of rating him in any way on a level with the moneygrubbers of the Mercato Nuovo— though the majority of even these servants of Mammon went to Mass at the appointed times, performed their Easter duties, and called for a priest at the end—it may pardonably be assumed that he looked after his profits as keenly as any other business man. Grumbling, he nevertheless did not oppose Philip—a point to be noted. The contemporary record of this crisis in a solid upper-class medieval Italian family with patrician connections is lamentably meagre, and a few of St. Philip's biographers, of whom there are at least fifty in various languages, tend to indulge themselves overmuch in legend and conjecture on this point, among others.

A brief recent "profile" of the saint by Fr. Luigi Maria Pazzaglia of his order[1] is a model for modern hagiographers in its judicious clarity and swift, shrewd sureness of touch, together with a graceful dash of humour. At seven centuries' distance we are quite unable to judge how far what seems like legend may be strictly factual. The thirteenth century moreover was no more—possibly a great deal less—credulous than the twentieth, of which a philosopher lately remarked that in no other age but ours have so many people believed what they could not possibly prove. In the pages that follow, any citations from legend will be clearly labelled as such and left at that. In the matter of St. Philip's miracles, mostly posthumous, the Church's ruling has (as also on private revelations) naturally been followed. One is not compelled to accept the authenticity of any miracle whatsoever, barring those revealed in Holy Writ; at the same time one is bound, Almighty God being omnipotent, to recognise their possibility. Those attributed to St. Philip which are testified by a cloud of eyewitnesses and recorded by lawyers are here accepted without question; obviously they happened.

It has not been deemed necessary to explain or defend the ethos of the religious life itself, there being infinitely more sources of enlightenment on this matter available in print in 1959 than there were in manuscript in the time

[1] *S. Filippo Benizi, nella Storia e nella Legenda.* Rome, 1953.

of St. Philip Benizi. Any order which has been in the world for seven hundred years will naturally have made a few minor adjustments in its mode of living, conformable to the necessities of the time. This does not apply, however, to the Rule in spirit or application.

II

DOCTOR OF MEDICINE

I.

THOUGH not in the first flight of the great mercantile families of medieval Florence which so skilfully blended blue or bluish blood with business capacity, or rapacity—such as the Pazzi, the Buondelmonti, the Frescobaldi, the Bardi, the Tosinghi, the Amidei, and half a dozen other precursors of the inimitable Medici—the Benizi, originally from Fiesole, were of gentle birth and qualified to wear arms: on a field of azure, *semée d'estoiles*, an eagle argent, displayed.

By 1233, the year of St. Philip's birth, they had given Florence twenty "priors", or chief city councillors, and one "gonfalonier", or Governor of the Republic. After Philip's death they were to serve the State still more for a couple of centuries. His father, Messer Giacomo dei Benizi, had married into one of the reigning families. His wife, Donna Albaverde, belonged to the Frescobaldi, a leading Guelf clan. He himself was a prosperous merchant, apparently a figure in the Guild (or "Art") of Apothecaries, importing drugs and spices from the East. The house in which St. Philip was born was later partly demolished, partly absorbed into the present Pitti Palace in the Via Guiccardini, formerly called the Via Benizi. In the eighteenth century, the Benizi having become extinct in the Renaissance and their in-laws the Frescobaldi having sold the house to the Guiccardini, the latter family placed a still-existing marble slab over the main entrance. It reminds the passer-by that "Saint Philip Benizi, who now receives in Heaven the honours you pay him, first saw the light in this house".

One or two notables less visibly qualified for Paradise stayed at the Frescobaldi palazzo in the Oltrano quarter. Charles of Anjou, King of Sicily, accompanying Pope Gregory X and the Emperor Baldwin II of Byzantium to Florence in 1273, was a guest for some weeks; Charles of Valois also stayed with the family during his visit of 1301. The Frescobaldi gave several soldiers of distinction and high officials to the Republic, administered, with the Bardi, the financial affairs of Philip the Fair of France and Edward II of England, and claim a fourteenth-century relative to whom the whole civilised world owes a debt immeasurable. Everyone acquainted with Boccaccio's *Life of Dante* knows how the sweet Tuscan lyrical poet Dino Frescobaldi, Dante's close friend, was able to rescue the first seven cantos of the *Divine Comedy* when Dante was driven into exile, and to convey them to him later at Lunigiana. Thus and thus only was Dante, who had deemed his manuscript lost for ever, encouraged to continue. The Frescobaldi had—or have, since they are apparently still in existence—much to be complacent about.

So (to resume), we may situate our saint clearly to begin with; a scion of the Florentine upper class, coming of what the Scots call "kennt folk". His background can easily be reconstructed in imagination. Messer Giacomo's house would lack nothing in the way of handsome, solid furnishings: massive carved credences and sideboards, a

sufficiency of fine linen and silver plate; comely tapes-
tries, possibly of Arras, on the walls; polished marble
floors in the principal rooms at least; curtains and bed-
hangings of figured silk or brocade; a house combining
the amenities of a comfortable home and, rather necessarily, a fortress, like some of the surviving Florentine
palazzi. The Benizis' parish church would presumably be
the medieval predecessor of the present San Felice, next
to which the Brownings lived later and into which,
apparently, they never poked their poetic noses. On the
nearby Ponte Vecchio the boy Philip must often have
lingered on the way to his tutor's house, looking at the
shops or gazing down on the river.

His parents were devoted and elderly and he was their
first child, arriving after years of prayer and a special vow
to Our Lady. There seems no reason to reject the story
that Donna Albaverde, very like St. Dominic's mother,
saw her expected child in due course in a dream, with a
flame on his brow. It is the first of the legends, handed
down on the authority, *circa* 1456, of a Florentine doctor
of canon and civil law named Paolo Attavanti of the
Servite Order, a man of piety and merit. The Benizi
family was still flourishing at the time, and Fra Paolo
doubtless recorded a family tradition. That Philip was
born, according to another story, at the precise hour on
Assumption Day in which Our Lady appeared to the
Seven Holy Brethren of Florence who founded the Servite Order is another matter, and Father Luigi Pazzaglia
pauses in an early page to consider it, with other legends
of saintly precocity, in the light of modern misgivings.
Are such stories statements of fact based on evidence now
lost, or merely poetry or folklore handed down the
centuries by uncritical biographers desirous of increasing

the fame of their saint? His conclusion is that whatever they may be, their authenticity is not an issue. Though possible in God's design, such marvels affect St. Philip's stature neither one way nor the other—*la grandezza di Filippo non è lì*. He was canonised not for a miraculous infancy but for spending a valiant life in the service of God and Our Lady of Sorrows. Content to rest on this sound judgment, we may pass on.

The boy Philip Benizi, then, grew up in the house by the Arno, much like other boys, no doubt, just as noisy and playful and moody, undoubtedly nearer to the Eternal. There is actually very little to record about his childhood or his adolescence, except that he had a worthy tutor for his earliest schooling. At the age of ten he is said to have recited daily the Little Office of Our Lady, which is not abnormal in a child of his period, and with "extreme devotion", which is not abnormal either. Some biographers add to his daily prayers the recitation of the Office for the Dead, the Litany, and the seven penitential psalms. To our own tepid age this might seem piety above the average in a small boy. It was not so in an age where ordinary rank-and-file Catholics, in England as elsewhere, often heard two or three Masses before breakfast and might, like St. Thomas More three centuries later, wear a hairshirt, an article rarely found in the average Catholic wardrobe to-day. It does not seem that an hour a day spent at prayers is incompatible with Philip's playing a good game of the contemporary version of hopscotch and teasing the little sister who arrived a year or two after him; just as the hard and dangerous and devoted life of a Welsh Jesuit of the seventeenth century did not affect Blessed Philip Evans's love of bowls, at which game he was an acknowledged master. But some of Philip's first

biographers are determined to endow him with aloof and
ethereal sanctity from the cradle. A later French one, the
sixteenth-century Father Germain Sardou, who turned
St. Philip's life into a long Latin sequence of dactyls and
spondees dedicated to Louis XIV, goes further and evolves
a picture of the boy which is refuted by all we know of
his temperament and character in the years of maturity;
a mirthless, morose child, spurning all boyish games,
"never wrinkling his nose with jests, never making any
uproar offensive to wellbred ears",

> Intorquet nullos naso crispante cachinnos,
> nec strepitus edit, mollis quos respuit auris ...

In fact a finished little prig, moving Father Pazzaglia to
testiness. Obviously Philip was a normal, healthy Italian
boy, joyously alive in every fibre of his being, at the same
time deeply religious and increasingly fond of books. We
see him emerging thus into adolescence, walking buoy-
antly, wearing the gay doublet and hose of his social degree with an air. He did not escape the common lot of
adolescents under an Italian sky. *Tenuabat*, says one of the
chroniclers briefly and significantly; he grew thin, he held
firm. The eighteenth-century poet Francesco Ercolani
embroiders this theme somewhat lavishly in an oratorio-
libretto, entitled *Le Metamorforsi della Verità* ("The Meta-
morphoses of Truth"), featuring, as we say to-day, the
Enemy laying his snares for the Beloved, "the youth so
dear to Heaven",

> il giovinetto
> al ciel così diletto ...,

with all the Loves and Sirens at his command. A flowery,
theatrical piece, recalling the elaborate painted ceilings of

the period. Truth herself, *La Verità*, a soprano or mezzo-soprano undoubtedly of commanding proportions, enters at the zenith of the struggle to sustain the angelic youth with an aria in *bel canto*, assuring him that the tempting visions of delight displayed by the Enemy are false and baneful mirages.

> Quei beni che vedete
> son pene e non diletti ...

The chorus supports her, *fortissimo*. The piece has a queer tinsel charm, baroque and rococo mingled, unconnected with reality of any kind, as evocative of eighteenth-century Italy as are, for some of us, the opening bars of Rossini's *La Gazza Ladra*. It would conceivably have raised St. Philip's eyebrows considerably had he ever heard of it.

All this is to anticipate slightly. The Philip we are contemplating is now about twelve years old, the age at which boys of his period were sent to a university, and his father has definite plans for him. Determined, it seems, to continue the Benizi line with his cherished only son and to checkmate any attraction towards the monastic life, doubtless already manifest, Messer Giacomo packed Philip off to the University of Paris, then the centre of the intellectual world.

A small difficulty presents itself. At the end of 1252 we find young Philip Benizi at the University of Padua, reading medicine in the faculty there and qualifying in due course, in accordance with the paternal plan. Why therefore, if Messer Giacomo Benizi's intention was to make his son a doctor, the youth should have spent four or five years beforehand taking an arts course at Paris is not clear, nor does any biographer shed light on it. His father may, after all, merely have wanted to give the boy a sound education.

Philip went up, at any rate, to the University of Paris. There is not much news of him there. Had he been entered for the theology schools he could have met Master Albert, "the Great", who arrived to qualify for his doctorate and lecture in 1240; also his tall, burly, brilliant pupil, Friar Thomas Aquinas, who himself took up his lectureship in 1252. Both men were the cynosure of the university and Philip might have known them. The vexing silence of all his biographers on this part of his early career is due, it seems, to two mishaps. The original pioneer Life in manuscript, the work of St. Alexis Falconieri, entrusted to Fra Pietro da Todi, eighth General, soon after Philip's death, disappeared without trace round about 1290, and a chronicle of the Servite Order by the same hand perished accidentally in a fire some time in the sixteenth century. There is of course no particular reason why Philip should have encountered either of his illustrious fellow-saints, or Roger Bacon either. The university was large, turbulent, and cosmopolitan, Philip was an ordinary foreign undergraduate, the faculties did not mix, and young Benizi seems not to have been the type who would run after celebrities; as these three certainly were, Aquinas above all. Did not a university ordinance of 1309 authorise poor students in extreme want to sell all their books except the Bible and the works of Friar Thomas (*Biblia dumtaxat et fratris Thomae operibus exceptis*)?

One pictures Philip likewise too devout and fastidious, and perhaps too frail, to indulge in the current university sport of brawling. Lusty black-gowned youth from all over Christendom, mainly grouped to begin with, and excluding the Orientals, in four "Nations"—France, Picardy, Normandy, and England, with later additions[1]— seems at times to have devoted most of its lesiure to creating uproar in the taverns, fighting the Provost's police, romping with the long-suffering night-watch, or settling international differences with fists, belts, and clubs. Jacques de Vitry gives us the thirteenth-century picture, looking somewhat down his nose:

> Because of the difference of their homes they dis-
> agree and are envious and insulting, and without shame
> they offer insult and contumely, saying that the Eng-
> lish are drunken and have tails, the French proud, soft,
> and womanish, the Germans mad and traitors and fair-
> weather friends. The Burgundians they deem brutish
> and slow, and thinking the Bretons fickle, they often
> throw in their teeth the death of Arthur. The Lombards
> they call avaricious, full of malice, and unwarlike, the
> Romans seditious, violent, and nail-biters, the Sicilians
> tyrannical and cruel, the men of Brabant men of blood,
> incendiaries and bandits, the Flemings prodigal, given
> over to feasting and soft as butter. And because of such
> wrangling they often proceed from words to blows.

Thus a ball-game one summer evening on the Pré-aux-Clercs, the university's sports ground, might flare up suddenly into a mass-battle fought all over the Left Bank. The Italians, it may be observed, come off pretty badly in De Vitry's catalogue; Philip Benizi would of course count as a Lombard. Twenty years before his arrival recurring top-level clashes between the civil power and the university, which derived authority directly from the

---

[1] The "Nation" of England included the Germans, the Swedes, and the Dutch.

Holy See, had evoked a Bull of Gregory IX whereby the university could deal with encroachments on its rights and privileges by employing a powerful weapon, the suspension of all lectures and all sermons in the churches of Paris. Since, finally, every student was a *clerc*, that is to say, in minor Orders, answerable under canon law only to ecclesiastical authority, a state of prevailing tension between the Rector Magnificus of the University and the Provost of Paris will not seem remarkable.

The arts course taken by Philip Benizi covered the seven "liberal arts", beginning with the *trivium*—grammar, rhetoric (including poetry and the elements of law), and dialectic—and proceeding with the *quadrivium*, namely mathematics, music, geometry, and astronomy. His college is difficult to discover. It must have been one of the existing French foundations. Colleges for the foreigners—Italians, Scots, Spaniards, Scandinavians, Greeks, and others—were part of the immense expansion of the next century, the Collège des Lombards for Philip Benizi's fellow-countrymen being founded by Andrea Ghini of Florence, Bishop of Arras, in 1333. The Arts Schools stood in the Rue du Fouarre, to which Dante alludes in the *Commedia*, though the story of his presence there for a short time is open to doubt.

Against this rich, tumultuous background we may attempt to visualise a slender Italian youth in a black academic gown. In maturity St. Philip seems to have been slim and a little under medium height; physically (as otherwise) of the type of St. John of the Cross, who was playfully nicknamed by St. Teresa "Senequita", Little Seneca, on account of his lack of inches and his characteristic gravity. Like any other foreigner abroad for the first time, he must have had a few bouts of homesickness.

Italians in particular were not over-popular in Paris at this period. The Lombard financiers and tax-farmers serving the Crown got into severe trouble with Louis IX for exploitation, and his successor Philip the Fair even expelled them for a time. We know that Philip Benizi was in constant touch with home during his stay, either by way of the postbags of the regular university couriers or through the Paris agents of his mother's people, the Frescobaldi, who did a great deal of business with the French. He must have seen plenty of Paris. Notre-Dame and the Sainte Chapelle, both fresh and gleaming white; St. Louis IX, King of France, walking by the river or dispensing justice under the famous elm of Vincennes; a flashing squadron of armoured feudal cavalry just returned from the Holy Land; the new hospitals of the Hôtel-Dieu and the Quinze-Vingts, near the Louvre, opened in 1254 for three hundred blind; the colleges, hostels, and halls already built and still building in the university quarter, of which the earliest was the Dix-Huit, founded in 1180 by the wealthy English pilgrim Josse de Londres on his return from Jerusalem; the tall new basilica of St. Geneviève, encasing her dazzling shrine; the churches, the markets, the fairs, the bridges, the crowds, the constant many-coloured processions, religious and secular, the perpetual bell-music—all that comely, noisy Gothic Paris with its towers and spires may have had as little effect on our young Florentine as it had on Friar Thomas Aquinas, now lecturing at the Priory of St. Jacques, whose well-known remark to a student must have been made round about this time.

"Master, how beautiful is this city of Paris! If only it belonged to you!"

"Yes, indeed, a beautiful city. But I would rather have at this moment the homilies of Chrysostom on St. Matthew."

Padua was a different business.

After four years in Paris, Philip Benizi seems to have left, at his father's orders, without taking his degree in arts. We do not know. His early biographers are loftily indifferent to personalia and dates of any kind. We may take it at any rate that the year 1252 finds Philip Benizi in residence at Padua and attending lectures in the Faculty of Medicine there.

Possessing as yet no faculty of theology (Urban V added this in 1363), the University of Padua, now thirty years old, could hardly compare with that of Paris, the intellectual centre and power-house of Christendom, though the Second Council of Lyons accorded Padua, with Bologna, equal status in 1274. But in the fields of jurisprudence and medicine, in which latter science its only rivals were Salerno and Montpellier, medieval Padua was celebrated, attracting students from all over Europe and from Germany in particular. By Shakespeare's time its faculty of arts had a reputation as well, it seems.

> Since for the great desire I had
> To see fair Padua, nursery of arts,
> I am arrived for fruitful Lombardy ...

In the mid-thirteenth century, however, law and medicine were lavishly enthroned at Padua and the Queen of Sciences took a back seat; which may be why Urban V took steps in the following century. Apparently there was only one professor of theology, probably installed in a back room, on the strength, as against seven professors of

law, two of medicine, and two of dialectics and grammar
—to-day called philology—respectively. Medicine being
widely practised by medieval clerics as well as laymen, it
would be unfair nevertheless to view the tutelary genius
of Padua at this period as the spirit of Chaucer's Doctor
of Physic, that typical Harley-Street figure, fussy over
diet though "his studie was but litel on the Bible". That
materialist streak traditional to the medical profession may
have been as detectable here and there in Padua notwithstanding. St. Anthony of Padua had died in 1231.

Graeco-Arabian medicine ruled all Europe; Galen and
Avicenna were every faculty's lodestars; not till the Renaissance was well under way would the medical science
of Arabia be denounced as the spawn of corrupt Greek
texts and dethroned in every progressive medical school
in favour of the redistilled essence of Galen and Hippo-
crates, both on the thirteenth-century curriculum at
Padua. It has been established that Philip Benizi's tutors
must have included three men of some eminence, the
doctors Zambonini, Giovanni, and Agno. In the branch
of surgery the latest textbook was the *Chirurgia Magna* of
Bruno di Longobardo, recently published.

It is customary to look down from a lofty height nowadays on medieval medicine. The thirteenth-century
physician followed Galen on the functions of the brain, in
which arterial blood charged with the vital force creates
"animal" spirits. He likewise distinguished four separate
"complexions" in man, the sanguine, the choleric, the
melancholic, and the phlegmatic, exhibited, drugs apart,
the healing powers of a mass of herbs and simples, and
tended to mix medical theory, like his successors till well
into the Renaissance, with a little astrology. Any breach
of the Church's ban on this superstition was avoided by

holding, with St. Thomas Aquinas and Dante, that planetary influences, if any, can be successfully challenged and combated by faith and reason. Surgery was the minor branch, though Mondino da Luzzi's work in practical anatomy became notable later in the century. The thirteenth-century physician declined to mend fractures, administer purges and clysters, bleed, cup, blister, or bind up wounds, leaving all such manual work to the barber-surgeon. Major operations he performed himself, presumably. It might be said, perhaps, that on the whole the medical profession in St. Philip's time probably contributed little more to the deathrate than its successor of to-day. Our distant forbears' frames were tougher, their nervous systems less sensitive and less coddled, their diet freer from deleterious matter, and their spiritual metabolism infinitely more suited to coping with the ills of life. If they often died younger than we, the medievals bore sickness with patience and had less terror of death than some of their posterity.

In 1253, little more than a year after his entrance, Philip Benizi left the University of Padua with his degree in medicine, conferred at the usual public ceremony amid (say Rucellai and other early biographers) unanimous applause. The usual medical course being one of three to five years, this points undoubtedly to a fair amount of medical reading in Paris, possibly as a hobby. The fact is there, in any case. A very skilful physician, *medicus peritissimus*; a man learned in medicine, *doctus in medicinalibus*— in support of such contemporary tributes, however lyrical they sound, there is the fact, once more, that on returning to his native city he at once set up a successful practice. His feat at Padua, however striking, is not unique, we may reflect. If it is deemed lawful to compare young Dr.

Benizi with a much later clerico-medical colleague who qualified as a Bachelor of Medicine in six weeks, Dom François Rabelais of the Benedictine Order, it may be judged that they possessed much the same brilliancy and that Dr. Filippo Benizi, had he continued in practice, might have contributed one of the leading names to Italian medicine, ranking with Fracastoro and Acquapendente and Fallopio and the other Renaissance masters of his country.

Heaven and his own ambition had other plans for him. It has not seemed necessary, during this brief survey of his first twenty years, to keep referring to the mainspring of his entire existence. Exposed like the rest of us to trials and temptations, he was a saint absolute and regardant.

There are saints in the calendar of many kinds, some born in sanctity in every century and some achieving it, in some cases after half a lifetime of storm and stress. The huge, rough, tough, violent-tempered soldier who became St. Camillus de Lellis, and has been called the father of the Red Cross and the field-ambulance, is an outstanding example at one end of the scale; examples of the "cradle-saint" at the other are plentiful enough. St. Philip Benizi is one of these latter, clad throughout life in that invisible armour which the Enemy is powerless to penetrate. Prayer came naturally to him from the beginning. Holy Writ was his normal reading, and a special devotion to the Mater Dolorosa drew him inevitably into a new order inspired by it. As Chesterton sang long after:

> The Seven Swords of her Sorrow held out their hilts
> like a challenge,
> The blast of that stunning silence as a sevenfold trumpet
> blew,

Majestic in more than gold, girt round with a glory of
  iron,
The hub of Her wheel of weapons; with a truth, beyond torture, true.[1]

Black and gold—it seems to be a particular devotional
expression of the South, blossoming under blue skies
rather than grey ones. The superb lament of the *Stabat
Mater* was composed by one of the leading poets of
Umbria, Jacopone da Todi, in Philip's lifetime. The
Marian poetry-cycle of the medieval North, on the other
hand, seems at times to celebrate primarily the joys of
Mary, in a blaze of light and colour:

> O quam glorifica luce coruscas
> Stirpis Davidicae regia proles![2]

There have been "psychological" and "climatic"
theories accounting for this difference in religious em-
phasis. Many of them omit the point that Servite devotion to the Sorrows of Mary—which are the Prophecy
of Simeon, the Flight into Egypt, the Loss of the Child
Jesus in Jerusalem, the Meeting on the Way to Calvary,
the Witnessing of the Crucifixion, the Taking-Down of
Christ from the Cross, and the Burial[3]—is neither morbid
nor morose. There will be few men of his age radiating
a serener joy all his life than Fra Filippo Benizi.

So there came a day when young Dr. Benizi knew his
real vocation, closed his case-books, and bade farewell to
library and dispensary, having made the final round of

---

[1] *The Queen of Seven Swords*. London, 1926.
[2] "With what a glorious light you shine,
  O royal Bud of David's line!"
                (Anon., eleventh century).
[3] The Feast of the Seven Dolours, September 15, granted to the Servite
Order in 1668, was extended to the Universal Church by Pius VII in 1814.

his patients and donned his medical gown for the last time. It came early in 1254. Dr. Benizi had been making his Easter duties at the historic abbey of Fiesole, five miles away. Saying his prayers there before a crucifix given, according to legend, by St. Peter to St. Romulus, first martyr-bishop of Fiesole, he was addressed, like St. Teresa, by an interior voice. It approved his aspirations and directed him to present himself to the Servants of Mary "on the high hill where they dwell". This was, and is, called Monte Senario, about eight miles north of Florence, where to-day a motorbus-service takes the pilgrim. It is a steep and airy place, desolate and secluded, where the seven Florentine citizens who founded the Servite Order retired in 1234. Their second priory is still intact. It offers—to quote the current guide-book of the *Touring Club Italiano*—"little of artistic interest", and was not intended to. A home-made liqueur which helps the community to exist, called *Gemma di Pino*, now mitigates any aesthetic despairs.

It is perhaps convenient here to leave Dr. Benizi a moment, still on his knees in the abbey of Fiesole, and turn to survey for a moment the order of which he is to become such an ornament.

2.

In *Romola*, by George Eliot—there are still readers of George Eliot—amid the long, brilliant, many-coloured procession of all the clergy, religious orders, civic dignitaries, and guilds of Florence escorting the miraculous image of Our Lady of Pity, the *Madonna dell'Impruneta*, to the Duomo in Savonarola's time, is seen "the unmixed black of the Servites, that famous Florentine order founded by seven merchants who forsook their gains to adore the Divine Mother". Which is as nearly accurate, probably, as could be expected from a distinguished Victorian agnostic.

Seven citizens of Florence certainly founded the Servite Order, though they were not all merchants and certainly did not adore Our Lady as divine, being prevented from so doing by reason and the Catholic religion alike. Their foundation was due to a vision which appeared to them in the chapel of the Laudesi attached to the church of Santa Reparata—the Duomo campanile covers its site—on the feast of the Assumption, 1233; whether after Mass or Vespers, in sunlight or dusk, is uncertain.

The Laudesi ("Praisers") were a lay confraternity, chief of the many existing in Florence at this time, with a membership of some two hundred. Amid all the vices and follies of their turbulent, bright-coloured city, all her troubles internal and external, amid the clash of steel and the chink of gold, the lepers and the assassins and the crazy Catharists, flourished a deep and mystical Christian devotion in every section of the community. The Laudesi, mostly recruited from the upper class, met regularly to sing hymns to Our Lady, recite her Office, and hear Mass and Vespers on her feasts. Seven of those present on August 15, 1233, were named Bonfiglio Monaldi, Alessio Falconieri, Manetto dell'Antella, Bartolomeo Amidei, Ricovero Uguccioni, Gherardo Sostegni, and Bonagiuncta Manetti respectively; all youngish members—twenty-seven to thirty-five—of the banking and mercantile aristocracy. To each and all of these on this memorable day, as they knelt in prayer after the rest of the Laudesi had dispersed, was suddenly vouchsafed a vision of Our Lady speaking to them in a blaze of light.

The manner of the vision is not known. It may have been visible to the eye or, perhaps, like those described by St. Teresa, an interior experience, *visión inteletual*. Each of the Seven saw it, at any rate; each believed himself at the time to be the only spectator; each heard Our Lady speak the same words:

"Leave everything. Put your life at my service."

And each answered instantly, "Yes, yes", after which the vision vanished. It was, as Montalembert has remarked, the age of chivalry, and in the very name— "Serfs of Mary"—of the order to be founded by these seven is expressed "the pride they felt, in that century of knightly dedication, in submitting themselves to the sweet yoke of the Queen of Heaven".[1]

When they had recovered what the world would call a state of normalcy they deputed tall, spare Bonfiglio Monaldi, their senior in years and their first superior in religion, to inform the chaplain of the Laudesi of what they had just seen and heard. The priest duly reported the wonder to his diocesan, Ardingo, Bishop of Florence. With the bishop's approbation at length the seven Laudesi began to settle their affairs before going about Our Lady's. They did not yet know what her orders might be. They did know, however, that their first obligation was to equip themselves for the service of the Mother of God by intensive prayer, fasting, and meditation in retirement.

Near the ramparts of Florence, on the verge of a large open space called the Campo di Marte, to-day boasting one of the biggest sports-stadia in Italy, was a remote, tumbledown old house, long empty, known as the Casa Camarzia. It seemed the ideal hermitage for the brethren's

[1] *Histoire de Sainte Élisabeth*, 1854.

present purpose. Having shed their silks and velvets, put on gowns of coarse grey or brown, and bidden their families farewell, they accordingly took up their quarters there and waited for Our Lady's instructions.[1] What little food they needed was begged from the charitable by two of the brethren in turn going from house to house. A charming legend allows one pair of them, calling at the house of Messer Giacomo Benizi, to be welcomed from his nurse's arms by a five-months-old child, the future St. Philip, with a cry of "Look! The Servants of Mary! Give them alms!" Who knows?

Inevitably the world began to discover the Casa Camarzia; and not merely the gapers, but many penitents and the devout. The Seven saw the quiet of their hermitage gone, and they dreaded the imminent uproar and buffoonery of the Carnival. They appealed to the Bishop of Florence, who came to their aid. Eight miles outside the city walls was a stretch of wild, rocky country belonging to the diocese. Its central feature, a hill called Monte Senario, some six hundred feet high, possesses several caverns and fissures very suitable for an ascetic retreat. Here some of the Seven were to stay the rest of their lives, rapt in communion with God, reciting the daily and nightly Office, enduring rigorous extremes of cold and heat, living on what food came to hand, and at first getting daily Mass from a priest, one Giacomo da Poggibonzi, who had accompanied them. From Ascension Day, 1234, Monte Senario was, so to speak, the GHQ of the Servite Order, as yet unborn. Down in the valley at the gates of Florence the Seven in due course established an outpost, a small and humble oratory called

[1] It is not known which of the Seven were married. Their wives would normally enter religion themselves.

Santa Maria di Cafaggio, where a handful of new brethren recited the Office and received alms. The Annunziata stands on the site.

On the evening of Good Friday 1240, as all the Seven on Monte Senario were in chapel, Our Lady's orders came at last. Visiting them as before, but this time in tears, and vested in black, she indicated their title, "The Servants of Mary", their rule, that of St. Augustine, and their habit, to be of black serge, symbol of devotion to the Seven Sorrows. The order, launched with the papal legate's permission in 1249, though as yet unofficially, soon began to spread over Italy, thence elsewhere. It had several vicissitudes before it yet, though some thousands strong before the end of the Middle Ages. In 1256 Innocent IV approved the foundation but thought fit to forbid all further exterior activities, considering the new order essentially a part of the Augustinian Order. His successor, Alexander IV, confirmed papal approval by a bull and restored Servite liberty. In 1274 consternation was caused by an edict of the Second Council of Lyons. On the ground that the growing number of orders and congregations was causing confusion—there are at least five times as many to-day—the Council suppressed all those founded since the Fourth Council of Lateran, 1215, except the Dominicans, the Franciscans, the Augustinians, and the Carmelites. A saving clause was attached, however. Foundations enjoying "special approbation" might continue. It was nevertheless not till 1304 that Benedict XI officially recognised the Order of Servants of Mary, who—according to the chronicler Pellati in 1492—had long since begun missionary work in India and Crete. In 1888, finally, the Seven Holy Founders, beatified in the seventeenth century, were canonised all together by Leo

XIII; an unique event in the history of the Calendar.

To-day as yesterday the Servite friar is simultaneously contemplative and active, mingling daily meditation, recital of the Office in choir, retreats, and other monastic obligations with such secular activities as preaching and parish organisation, education, care of the aged poor, home and foreign missions, and the publication of books and periodicals. From the Middle Ages onward the order flourished extensively in Italy and spread to Germany, France, Hungary and Poland, with outposts in the East. For some reason unknown, so many contemporary religious orders all over Christendom having begun in Italy, the Servites never appeared in pre-Reformation England, though they have one or two English names on their medieval rolls. It was not till 1864 that two Italian friars founded in London, with Archbishop Manning's blessing, the first English Servite Province, now embracing six priories in England and one in Scotland, with six convents for women, all wholly native.[1] In the United States there are now two provinces with about thirty priories and two hundred priests; one of the pioneers being the same Father Morini who did so much to found the English Province. In eighteenth-century France the order suffered greatly from the Commission reducing religious houses in Louis XV's reign, and was finally stamped out by the Revolution, to start again in the 1920's in the diocese of Versailles. To-day the Servites, grouped in twelve provinces, one rectorate, and ten commissiarats, have priories in Italy, Spain, England, Ireland, Belgium, Austria, Hungary, the United States, and Canada, and many missions in South America and Africa, where Swaziland is especially their territory; eighteen countries

[1] Gerard M. Corr, O.S.M., *Servites in London*, Newbury, 1952.

in all. There is an International Servite College at Rome. The Servite Second Order of enclosed nuns has founda- tions in several countries, including one at Bognor Regis. The Sisters of the Third Order, or *Mantellate*, founded by St. Giuliana Falconieri, are more numerous to-day than ever in their history. There is finally a Servite Third Order for lay people of both sexes, as with the Domini- cans and Franciscans; to this priests may also belong. The Order has so far added to the Roman Calendar eleven canonised saints and several *beati*.

With which we may return to Fiesole to find young Dr. Filippo Benizi, just risen from prayer, striding out into the sunshine with a joyful heart.

III

THE BLACK HABIT

I.

IT was now not possible for a layman to attach himself to the community on Monte Senario. Apart from having two well-loved parents to inform and console, Philip Benizi had to seek admission to the noviciate. He returned home next morning, stopping for Mass in the oratory at Cafaggio, alongside the city walls. During the Epistle at Mass, which recounted the preachings and miracles of St. Philip the Evangelist, he heard his interior call ("Philip! Philip!") unmistakably repeated. An illumination followed; seemingly an interior one, a vision of the Teresian kind. As Philip saw himself sinking into a frightful swamp, beset by perils seen and unseen, the black sky was suddenly flooded with sunshine and the Queen of Angels enthroned, in mourning garb, in a chariot of gold, was speaking to him, repeating the words of Acts 8: 29: "Go near; join thyself to this chariot." And she seemed then to beckon him, holding out the Servite habit. As he approached the vision it faded. He remained on his knees long after the congregation had dispersed, absorbed in ecstasy.

An elderly laybrother attending to his duties—it was St. Alexis Falconieri, one of the founders and Philip's first biographer, now in his fifties—appeared at length and approached him. It was the time for shutting the church doors, in the traditional Italian fashion, during the fiercest of the afternoon heat.

"Brother, Mass is over long since."

There was no response from the kneeling figure. He spoke again, touching Philip on the shoulder.

"We are about to close, brother."

With some difficulty Philip Benizi came to himself, fixing the laybrother with a look of bedazed reproach.

"God forgive you, Brother Alexis. You've brought me back from the very gates of Heaven."

And swiftly recovering his wonted amiability he took his leave and went on across the Arno to announce an irrevocable decision.

How Messer Giacomo Benizi received the news is no-where described. Whatever his disappointment he was a good Catholic, not wholly preoccupied with his banking-account. We may surmise that Donna Albaverde held her only son close and wept, but there was no with-standing a call from God. Filippo's young sister Giovanna must have been as glad as he. Her own desire, it is re-corded, was to take the veil. After her brother's departure she was prevailed on to marry one Forte da Sommaia. After his death, having given him a son, himself to enter the Order, and a daughter, Giovanna entered the Servite Third ("Mantellate") Order, and died years later in the odour of sanctity.

His parents duly gave Filippo their blessing. Having passed the remainder of that day and night in his room, re-experiencing the vision and rapt in prayer for hours, he sped early through the opaline hush of a Florentine summer morning to call on the Servites of Cafaggio. Here, having made his thanksgiving before Our Lady's picture in the chapel, he knocked at the priory door and was taken into the parlour, where the prior at length joined him. He was the doyen of the founders, St. Bonfiglio Monaldi, a man of fifty-six, well known for prudence and sanctity. Before long Philip was on his knees, begging for admission to the Order of the Servants of Mary.

It might have been a temporary fit of emotionalism, as the prior was well aware.

"Son, you need to be very strong of heart, and resolute, and faithful. This is a great and a difficult matter."

Filippo Benizi was in fact the ideal postulant. There is no set pattern of aspirants to the religious life; to-day as in any century a monk or friar may know plenty about the noisy world of men before deciding to turn his back on it. The Prior of Cafaggio was surveying a young man of science who had met many sorts of men and was moreover trained in exact observation of what medieval medicine called the Microcosm, the physical human mechanism. It cannot have taken him long—he undoubtedly knew Philip's family background—to discern his quality and sincerity and latent holiness. He proceeded briefly to expound the *raison d'être* of the Servite Order, now nearly twenty years old, and the symbolism of the habit of black serge. As an eyewitness of Our Lady's two apparitions Fra Bonfiglio Monaldi could speak with authority.

"You doubtless ask why Our Lady, instead of being vested gloriously, appeared to us in mourning garb. It was to remind us of the grief above all other griefs which she endured while witnessing the sufferings and death of her divine Son on Calvary. The black habit is worn by us, her servants, in remembrance of those sorrows, to honour which our order was founded on Monte Senario. It recalls to us perpetually the desolation of that dear mother, our mistress, and exhorts us constantly to the life of penance to which we are pledged. It is our distinguishing mark among other religious orders, given to us by Our Lady herself."[1]

They talked together a long time, so long that when the refectory-bell rang they were astonished to discover what time it was. The day was a Friday, kept in memory of the Passion as a rigid fast under the Servite rule and admitting only one short meal of bread and vegetables, taken at the hour of None, or 3 p.m. After this refection, which Philip shared with the community, and after the grace and the *Salve Regina* had been recited, a conference ensued in which the aims, objects, hardships, and compensations of the Rule were fully discussed for a would-be postulant's benefit. When this was over Philip Benizi knelt before them all with outstretched arms and begged them to admit him into their order. "My heart is ready to burst with joy when I think of the religious state.", he said. "I beseech you, fathers, to receive me in the arms of your compassion, since our dear Lord and his blessed mother have deigned to call me." And he repeated what he had already assured the prior, namely that he was ready and eager to serve as a laybrother for the rest of his life.

This raised a problem, the only one. To set a young man of Philip's attainments to sweep floors, wash dishes, chop wood, and answer the door thenceforth seemed to St. Bonfiglio, as to the others, as to anyone, a great waste. On the other hand, a course of such disciplinary value would do a novice of quality no harm. St. Alexis, a man of wealth, had chosen it for life. The prior therefore

---

[1] Like the historians of Greece and Rome, the early Philippine chroniclers do not report verbatim, but give a précis.

granted Philip's desire for the time being and left the rest
to God. The new postulant was put through the customary tests before being admitted to the noviciate. They
embraced tasks menial, arduous, and disagreeable. Cheerful humility carried him through triumphantly, and after
a much shorter probation than usual Filippo Benizi was
clothed by the prior in full chapter, during the recital of
the psalms, antiphons, and prayers pertaining, with the
coarse black leather-girdled tunic, scapular, and cape of a
novice-laybrother of the Servants of Mary. It is the rule
for novices to take another Christian name. Since Philip's
interior voice had on four occasions addressed him as
"Philip", he preferred and was permitted to keep his
baptismal one.

In pace, in idipsum ... Not one of the merchant-princes of
Florence can have slept that summer night, in silk sheets
on swansdown, behind damask curtains in a great carved
and gilded bed, as the Servite laybrother Filippo Benizi
slept till Prime on his hard, narrow pallet, after hours of
absorption in prayer and thanksgiving, wrapped in "that
innocence and liberty of soul that come to those who have
thrown away all preoccupation with themselves and
their own ideas and judgments and opinions and desires,
and are perfectly content to take things as they come to
them from the hands of God, and through the wishes and
commands of their superiors";[1] or waked to a more
crystalline and happier dawn.

2.

One of St. Philip's biographers, Fra Jacopo Tavanti, a
celebrated general of the order in the sixteenth century,

---

[1] Thomas Merton, *The Seven-Storey Mountain*, 1948, III, 4. (Published in
Great Britain under the title *Elected Silence.*)

sketches a pen-portrait of the new laybrother based on a living tradition. Cheerfulness, humility, and unremitting energy in every task set him from dawn to dark, all for the love of God, are what one might expect. There is an interesting passage recalling the Latin verses, quoted in Miss Waddell's *The Wandering Scholars*, on the loving care of Paulinus, ex-senator and priest, for the shrine of St. Felix at Nola nine centuries earlier.

> Every time he went into chapel he looked around with keen attention to see that everything there was clean and polished; the altars decorated as they should be, the pavement swept and washed, the sacristy in order, the flower-vases properly garnished ... And having performed everything ordered of him he was always to be found kneeling at prayer.

It was inevitable that Florentine gossip and curiosity should bring visitors flocking to Cafaggio. Before very long the prior judged it advisable, at Fra Filippo's own request, to send him up to Monte Senario for a space.

It was a more rugged journey from Pratolino, at the foot, than it is to-day, the mountain being then almost inaccessible and covered with woods, boulders, rocks, and thickets, with only a few rough tracks. On the strip of level ground near the top, partially cleared by the Founders, stood two or three wooden huts and a wooden oratory, forming their first priory. How many of the original Seven were still in residence there, or the then strength of the community, is not recorded. On taking the black habit the Founders had dropped family names and were now and thenceforth known as the Frati Bonfiglio, Bonagiuncta, Manetto, Sostegno, Amideo, Uguccione (or

Ugo), and Alessio.[1] The then Prior of Monte Senario, Fra Amideo, an accomplished judge of men, discerned the new laybrother to be of the right stuff and set him, in the intervals of a full and strenuous spiritual discipline of the utmost austerity, to digging and clearing. To these rigours, varied when his turn came by the eight-mile tramp into Florence and back, whatever the weather, to beg alms from house to house, Fra Filippo of his own accord added more by asking permission to pray, read, meditate, and live, when not at work or in choir, alone in a nearby cave.

As with St. Ignatius at Manresa three centuries later, and a number of other saints in every century down to the eighteenth, when cave-dwelling ceased, this challenge to the Enemy was soon taken up. From the trials of the next four years Fra Filippo emerged unscathed. On the severities to which he subjected his body—the rigorous fasting, the hair-shirt, the scanty meals of herbs and roots, the minimum of sleep after vigil and recitation of the whole night Office, and that sleep taken till dawn on the bare rocks, the constant scourge—on all this Fra Luigi Pazzaglia remarks that if such discipline seems to us inhuman and exaggerated, and even savage, it certainly did not seem so to the men of St. Philip's time, when the Passion of Christ was the centre of Christian meditation. "Meditating the Passion, the medievals were moved to sympathy in the realistic sense of the word—to suffer with their suffering Christ, to crucify themselves with Him." That mystical medieval intensity in sharing the pains of Christ is not easy to comprehend to-day. Whether Fra Filippo was submitting himself equally to penance for

[1] Rossi (*Alessio M., O.S.M.*), *Manuale di Storia dell'Ordine dei Servi di Maria.* Rome, 1956, Appendice III.

personal sins of adolescence is not known. Some of his biographers tend to assume it.

Towards the end of 1258 the third Servite General, Bl. Giacomo of Siena, deemed him sufficiently an exemplar of the Servite ideal to be sent to the new priory at Siena for a space. Accompanied, as the Rule directs, by a brother-friar, Fra Vittore, Fra Filippo consequently set forth, taking the road to Florence and staying a day or two on his way, by permission, at his parents' house. Of his homecoming it is reported that it gave all concerned such happiness and cordial comfort, *tanta letizia e cordial conforto*, as can hardly be described, though perhaps Messer Giacomo's glumness may not have immediately been broken down. It was not the last time his family would see Filippo, since he returned to Florence from his travels more than once or twice. But to their life he no longer belonged, and they must have realised it.

At Siena the brethren discovered before very long, as Fra Vittore had already discovered during a discussion on the road with a couple of chance-met Dominicans, that the modest laybrother from Florence was a scholar of some calibre with more than a smattering of theology. The incident is not unpicturesque. Nearing the gates of Siena two Dominicans from Germany overtook a couple of trudging religious of unknown breed, garbed in dusty black with leather girdles and shouldering a sack apiece, and inquired, curiously, and perhaps not without a touch of condescension—the *Summa* was not yet published, but the expertise of the Friars Preachers was already a byword —who and what they might be. "We are", Fra Filippo informed them, "natives of this country, and we call ourselves the servants of the most glorious Virgin, of whose mourning we wear the livery. We follow the apostolic way and live under the rule of the holy doctor Augustine." A theological discussion was very soon under way. The Dominicans marvelled at Filippo's combination of knowledge, skill in dialectic, and religious exaltation; he seemed to them another Stephen, "full of the Spirit and of divine grace". When they had sufficiently gone on, Fra Vittore, hitherto struck dumb and rolling astounded eyes, burst into a cry. "*Carissimo fratello mio*, don't call yourself a simple laybrother any more! You can't deny what I've just heard with my own ears." To which Filippo anxiously replied, "I beg you, *carissimo*, to mention this incident to nobody."

"That I will certainly not promise", retorted Fra Vittore. "Your gifts are of use to me, to our brethren, to our order, and to all the Church of Jesus Christ."

Nor, though repeatedly implored as they entered Siena, did he keep silence. Soon after Filippo's arrival his prior, himself sufficiently impressed, was writing to the General. The order was rapidly expanding and needing more priests. Before very long the laybrother Filippo was directed to prepare himself to enter Holy Orders, as the Servite Rule then allowed.[1] Stifling considerable apprehension and dismay, he obeyed. On Holy Saturday, 1259, in Santa Reparata, Florence, at the hands of Bishop Giovanni Mangiadoro, Fra Filippo Benizi was consecrated to the priesthood of the Universal Church, and a few weeks later sang the High Mass of Pentecost in the chapel on Monte Senario, the scene of the vision of Good Friday evening, 1240. To-day the low oblong chapel of the Founders, adorned in the early eighteenth century with marbles, frescoes, and an imposing reliquary of a martyr

[1] In later years laybrothers would require a papal dispensation for this purpose.

from the Roman Catacombs, forms the south transept of the Priory church, long since made dusky by surrounding buildings. When Fra Filippo Benizi sang his first Mass there it was exactly as it had been when, nineteen years before, Our Lady had appeared, garbed in black and bathed in tears, as if newly descended from the hill of Calvary, and escorted by angels bearing the sacred implements of the Passion, the lance, the nails, and the crown of thorns, displaying the Rule of Augustine, clearly superinscribed with the words "Servants of Mary", and carrying palms of glory and reward.

The emotions of the celebrant at the moment of consecration may well be imagined. Many of those present believed that they heard angelic voices joining in the *Sanctus*. In Todi over the border in Umbria at this moment was a twenty-nine-year-old lawyer-poet, Jacopone Benedetti by name, subsequently a Friar Minor, who was to be inspired by rapture hardly less intense to what Léon Bloy calls the most glorious flowering of sixteen centuries of the Latin tongue—that Plaint of Blessed Mary the Virgin, *Planctus Beatae Mariae Virginis*, commonly known as the *Stabat Mater*, ever since the chief hymn of the Servite Office.

> Eja! Mater, fons amoris,
> Me sentire vim doloris,
> Fac ut tecum lugeam!

Here, cries Bloy, is the true poetry of God—and there are still imbeciles who call Latin a dead language![1]

Fra Filippo was now to begin the travels of a lifetime. Chosen by St. Bonfiglio at the chapter-general at Pente-

---

[1] *Belluaires et Porchers*, 1905. Jacopone's authorship of the *Stabat* is now recognised by the most competent authorities.

cost as his *socius*, colleague, or travelling-companion, he accompanied him in a visitation of the Servite houses of Tuscany and Umbria. We next hear of him at the end of 1261, once more at Monte Senario, attending the dying-bed of the aged ex-general; second of the Founders to die, St. Buonagiuncta having preceded him by three years. Not long afterwards we find Fra Filippo again at the priory in Siena, having been appointed Master of Novices there.

His rules, based on self-abnegation, for the training of youth to the religious life, written down with those already in use, were published later during his general-ship. A few directions for deportment may be quoted as redolent of their age, of the cloister, and of Italy:

> During processions, let the novice take heed to the companion with whom he is paired.
>
> In drinking let the cup be held with both hands, the novice being seated.
>
> Let the novice in all humility hold in honour the habit given us by the Blessed Virgin, and let him frequently kiss it.
>
> Let novices take great care of books, clothes, and other property of the priory.
>
> Let them not speak at times or in places forbidden.
>
> Let them not speak of the absent, unless it be in their favour.
>
> If a novice should scandalise [i.e., incite to sin by any word or action with the appearance of evil] another, he shall prostrate himself at his brother's feet until pard-oned and raised by him from the ground.

The rule concerning the cup, common to most of the ancient orders, refers to earthenware bowls used at table in monastic houses, and is said to have originated at Monte Cassino in St. Benedict's time. The novice—to conclude St. Philip's rules—must be free of debt before profession, and sufficiently instructed in psalmody, the offices of the Church, and all other things pertaining to the religious life. He is not, except under necessity, to be sent on a journey of any distance, is not eligible for any office in the community, and is to make frequent use of the discipline, or scourge. Novices' lay clothing must not be given away before profession except with their consent, and they are not to be candidates for ordination before being professed. The spiritual training they received from Fra Filippo was, as may be judged, deep, thorough, and in the spirit of the order. As a Master of Novices he may be assumed to have ruled less by severity than by *epikeia*, the sweet reasonableness urged by St. Paul. As in any age, there must have been one or two hard cases among the novices at Siena; evincing special restlessness, perhaps, just before some festa of the dimensions of the much-later *Palio*, when the top drummers of all the wards of Siena would be practising on summer evenings.

In 1264 Fra Filippo is seen at Cafaggio, assisting St. Alexis with final preparations for the building of the Santissima Annunziata, which began at last in the December of that year. In 1264 likewise he was chosen as *socius* to the fourth general, St. Manetto. At Pentecost 1267, June 5, finally, at the chapter-general held in Florence, having vainly and earnestly begged the definitors and all his brethren to find somebody better, Fra Filippo Benizi was unanimously elected fifth general of the Order of Servants of Mary.

IV

THE GENERAL

I.

LIKE that of any other religious order of its antiquity in the Catholic Church, the seven-hundred-year-old administrative machinery of the Servites has needed relatively little readjustment to work smoothly down the ages. What is called "the democratic element" may be everywhere recognised in it, though democracy is accorded no worship and is not its basis. The vow of obedience, subjecting every member of the order personally to the Holy See and to his superiors, is naturally of more importance.

Every office of weight within the order is elective. In each priory the votes of the conventual chapter, composed of the prior and all but the youngest friars, decide all matters of moment to the community. The prior, who rules for three years, is elected at the provincial chapter by the votes of the provincial, the assistant provincial, the definitor-general, and four definitors, all seven elected by this chapter as well. Votes at a provincial chapter are exercised by these seven officials and a number of other delegates, representing between them every Servite house in their province, with the foreign missions pertaining. Above the provincial chapter comes the general chapter, composed of the General of the Order, the ex-General, the Procurator-General, the provincials of all the provinces, with their assistants, the four councillors of the general council, one definitor-general from each province, and the superior of each foreign mission territory. It is the general chapter which, every six years, elects the general and his council. The order observes the three monastic vows. Its rule for friars and nuns alike is essentially, as already observed, that of St. Augustine—the basis of the Augustinian, Dominican, and Jesuit rules equally—adapted to the Servite genius.

The great African Doctor left no formal directive or schedule. In a brief sequence of ardent pages he merely indicates the essentials of the religious life, based on Holy Writ: love of God, love of the brethren, love and pity and charity for all mankind, the rich and great included; a communal existence, voluntary poverty and renunciation, constant prayer and fasting, fraternal correction, obedience and respect for superiors, and so forth. The rest St. Augustine leaves to those concerned to work out for themselves, and with all their differences the common source of all rules thus derived is evident. As the latest of the five mendicant orders, dependent on the alms of the faithful for every bodily need, the Servites had the same aims as the Dominicans, Franciscans, Augustinians and Carmelites, their predecessors. "To the Mendicants", observes an eminent Oxford historian, "the calm, monotonous round of solemn service was but a subordinate object; the end of their existence was the salvation of souls."[1] The past tense and the word "monotonous", twin tokens of a characteristic survey from above and afar, being duly discounted, this may be taken as a working definition still.

[1] Rashdall, H., *Universities of Europe in the Middle Ages*, Oxford, 1936. The Servites retained a right to property—a legal point which would be of some importance in due course.

On the Rule of St. Augustine, then, the Servites had already based, and recorded in writing, regulations or "constitutions" suitable to their own concept of the religious life. In 1249 a general chapter presided over by St. Bonfiglio on Monte Senario, now and henceforth under the immediate protection of the Holy See, had defined such matters as fasting, abstinence, recital of the Divine Office, the scope of a prior's authority, the material and shape of the Servite habit, even the kind of hard mattress furnishing the cells. Fresh decrees approved by episcopal and papal authority were issued between 1255 and 1260, in which year the growing order was divided into two provinces, the Tuscan and the Roman. In July, 1263, a brief of Urban IV authorised the elections of priors-general by the general chapter. By the time Fra Filippo Benizi succeeded Fra Manetto of the comely and delicate aspect, *bello di aspetto e di complessione delicata*, it seemed that the Servite Order was all-but-formally recognised by Rome already. But the time was not yet.

It was during Fra Filippo's early days as prior-general that the first of what have been called the three "classic" miracles of his lifetime took place. In Servite churches everywhere this has ever since been commemorated by the blessing and distribution of tiny loaves of white bread before High Mass on St. Philip's Day, August 23; a ceremony as exclusive to the order as the distribution of roses before High Mass on Rosary Sunday is to the Dominicans. The miracle took place at Arezzo in Tuscany. Continuous recent fighting between local Guelfs and Ghibellines had wasted the countryside, trampling down cornfields, vineyards, olive-groves, and orchards for miles around. Ghibellines expelled from Florence had taken to highway-robbery in the district likewise.

There was in consequence a widespread food shortage.

Summoned to the Servite house in Arezzo, Fra Filippo found the brethren literally starving, their normally charitable fellow-townsmen having had no crusts to spare for some days past. When the bell rang at None for the principal meal of the day, as the Rule required, the friars filed nevertheless into refectory and took their places at bare tables. Here Fra Filippo questioned the prior again in their presence.

"Have you done all you can? Have you sent out two of the brethren to beg alms, according to the custom of our order?"

"Reverend Father," the prior answered, "this morning I sent out nearly all of them. The people of Arezzo are always ready to help us, but they cannot give what they have not got."

Fra Filippo briefly addressed the community on the topics of faith and hope. "Do you not remember what Holy Scripture has to say concerning the compassion of Almighty God? Do you not recall the sending down of manna in the desert and Our Lord's feeding of the five thousand? Have you forgotten likewise that Our Lady is known throughout the world as the Mother of Grace? Let us go into chapel together, not doubting that we shall see the wonders of God's loving-kindness and mercy before this day is out."

They preceded him into their chapel in the customary order, two by two, pale with hunger. Kneeling with them before a statue of Our Lady and the Child which is still preserved at Arezzo, Fra Filippo prayed aloud with and for all of them in their extremity. While they were thus engaged, an hour later, two loud knocks were heard at the priory door. The prior and two friars hastened to open it. There was nobody there, and nobody anywhere in sight, but two large baskets stood at the door, filled with good wheaten loaves. An ideal subject for Andrea del Sarto and other painters a couple of centuries later: the wide-open door, the empty street, the wan black-clad friars gazing speechless at each other in the afternoon sun.

There was no more famine in Arezzo, but there was trouble in Bologna, where the Servites were suffering from the heavy hand of Vicar-General Ottaviano, bishop of that city, who had refused to extend to them the privileges restored to the regular orders by Alexander IV, following Innocent IV's rigorous curtailment of the same fourteen years previously. Ruling that the Servites, an order not recognised as yet by Rome, were not entitled to such restoration, the Vicar-General of Bologna forbade them to admit the laity to their church on Sundays or holy days, to preach before the parochial Mass, to hear the confessions of the laity, or to bury them. If any parishioner of San Blasio, in which parish their priory was, entered the Servites' church during any service, it was to be suspended forthwith. The friars had no right to any gifts made in that parish, any legacy or endowment made to them was to be handed over immediately to the parish priest, and they were not to ask or receive alms within the parish for any object whatsoever. Whether this was secular high-handedness of a traditional kind or due merely to the desire to vex and harry is not clear. On arrival in Bologna Fra Filippo at once called a chapter in the Servite house to elect procurators to put their case either to the Pope or a legate. They elected two Servites, from Florence and Siena respectively, and a secular canon. A deed of confirmation was signed on July 8, 1267, and

Fra Filippo proceeded to Viterbo, where the new Pope Clement IV, consecrated in that city two years previously, was in residence.

The Pope was in Viterbo, with the Curia, because he was prevented by Ghibelline force from going to Rome. The papal palace on the main piazza in Viterbo is not so well known as the palace at Avignon. It is a fine example of thirteenth-century Tuscan Gothic with an airy arcaded loggia and a comely consistory hall. Here, four years hence, in 1271, the roof would be taken off and the cardinals locked in and put on short rations by the "Captain of the People" in an ineffective attempt to force them to come to a decision about Clement IV's successor. As the ex-*socius* of St. Manetto, the late Servite General, Fra Filippo was well enough known to Clement IV, who esteemed him highly. His business with the Holy Father was to have his election as general confirmed, and, if possible, to have his order accorded full recognition and all due privileges. Clement IV at once confirmed the generalship after a formal report on its validity from Cardinal Ottobuono Fieschi, protector of the order. The other matter would take considerable time. Having a visitation on hand, Fra Filippo was content, after long consultation with the Cardinal-Protector, to leave it in his hands. It was to be thirty-seven years before authority finally signed and sealed.

How long the visitation of some twenty present houses of the four Italian provinces—Tuscan, Roman, Emilian, and Romagnolan—lasted is not recorded. St. Philip's *socius*, Fra Lottaringo della Stufa, later enrolled among the order's *beati* in accordance with tradition, was a good classical scholar and had known his General from childhood. They may be pictured as two black-garbed figures tramping the roads together during the cooler hours, deep in devotional talk; sandalled, sunburned, and dusty, or equally soaked and mudsplashed, each with his sack and staff. During the furnace-heat peak of the Italian summer afternoon they would rest under the nearest clump of trees, conversing, praying, or meditating. The same kind of creaking wagons drawn by the same slow-pacing beautiful fawn-coloured oxen with the gracefully-curving horns we see on country roads to-day would be overtaken and passed, with the same kind of waggoner snoring in the shade. Except that the main roads of Italy are now wide and smooth and exhibiting, notably along the great Via Emilia, a terrifying procession of enormous lorries thundering at daemonic speed, the countryside would look much the same: the cypresses, the vineyards, the olive-groves, the high hills, with a sparkling level snowline as the travellers neared the Gran Sasso; the hill-towns of the Marche on their distant crags, each with its campanile and towers rising above a huddle of red roofs, each clear as a miniature in a Book of Hours; the vast blue sky over all.

Fra Filippo and his *socius* returned to Viterbo after this visitation, perhaps with a group of carefully-selected recruits for the East—his special dream, as it had been St. Manetto's—to seek the Pope's blessing. An oft-repeated tradition that these Servite pioneers in the mission-field were martyred for Christ before long by Tartars in Armenia is difficult to confirm. It may well be so, but there is no official record.[1] There would be plenty of Servite missionary activity in succeeding centuries, our own above all. However, having presented his recruits to the Holy Father, General Fra Filippo and his *socius*

[1] Rossi, *Manuale di Storia*, etc., cap. v ("*Missioni tra gli Infedeli*").

returned to Florence for the important business of drawing up the Constitutions.

This work, constantly interrupted by other duties, was to take some months. As already observed, its foundation was the Rule of St. Augustine. Conferences with the remaining Founders of the order and knowledgeable religious, the collection of records during visitations, study of the practice of other orders, due regard to tradition and local customs, and his own inspiration and experience, supplied the material for the twenty-two chapters of what are called "St. Philip's Constitutions". The original manuscript is no longer in existence, and a copy in the possession of St. Alexis vanished likewise towards the year 1310; it is apparently not easy, according to Rossi, to distinguish St. Philip's own contributions. The constitutions cover everything from the proper Masses and Offices of Our Lady to be said or sung in Servite churches and chapels throughout the year down to the matter of the Friday fast. The Roman Breviary alone is to be used. In an age when a great amount of latitude was permitted in this matter, with a score of different uses and breviaries in existence all over Christendom, this adherence to the Roman use was, so to speak, a hallmark, like the devotion to Our Lady which is the keynote of the Servite Offices.

It is interesting to find, in these early Constitutions, the primitive form of the *Ave Maria*, as recited after the *Pater Noster* at the beginning of each of the Servite Hours. The Hebdomadarius or officiating friar of the week begins:

Ave, Maria, gratia plena, Dominus tecum ...

And the brethren answer:

... Benedicta tu in mulieribus, et benedictus fructus ventris tui.

Not till 1461, following St. Bernadine of Siena's preachings on the Holy Name, and in accordance with a decree of the Chapter of Treviso, did the order add "Jesu" to "ventris tui". The rest of the *Ave* as said to-day—"Sancta Maria, Mater Dei, ora pro nobis", etc.—is still later, being first found in a breviary of the Camaldo-lese Order printed at Venice in 1514.

The constitutions duly drawn up, the general's next duty was to submit them to a general chapter, by whom they would be in due course transmitted to the Pope. The general chapter of 1268 was held at Pistoia, under the Appenines north of Florence, at the order's second oldest house. Here, having duly recited the *Salve Regina* and de-livered a discourse on Psalm CXVIII, *Beati immaculati*, Fra Filippo proceeded to read out his work, which was im-mediately approved. Four new definitors were then pro-posed and elected according to the form. No sooner had they been confirmed in office than Fra Filippo, to the sur-prise and dismay of the whole assembly, handed them his general's badge of office, praying them to accept his resignation.

He had had a year of multifarious business and intense activity and was now, he explained, longing for obscurity, prayer, penance, contemplation, and solitude with God. It was not an unreasonable plea. He had done a great deal for the order, and the contemplative half of the Servite ideal had been perforce in eclipse most of the time. The definitors, nevertheless, were proof against argument, pleading, and even tears. Only a theologian is qualified to judge how far they were justified in compelling their general to sacrifice his contemplative longings to the general weal. He submitted at length with his usual humility and allowed himself to be confirmed again in the generalship. It was then, apparently, when the chapter was over, that the Enemy took advantage of his self-sacrifice to assault him with anxieties, doubts, alarms, weariness, and disgust at the prospect of yet another period of a responsibility and rule for which he still held himself unfitted.

After some days of agitation Fra Filippo left for Viterbo, accompanied by his *socius*, Fra Lottaringo, with the object of asking Clement IV's permission to resign. At the audience Fra Lottaringo, who had already discovered his superior's intention and done his utmost to make him change his mind, begged the Holy Father almost in tears not to listen to him, there being no man in the order comparable in wisdom, prudence, and virtue. A few words of encouragement and exhortation from Clement ended the matter. Fra Filippo humbled himself once more and obeyed. Naturally, the approval of the constitutions could not be so quickly decided. Leaving a procurator to attend to this, Fra Filippo left Viterbo and continued his visitations.

It was a month or so later, on the road from Arezzo to Perugia, that a messenger from Monte Senario caught up with him. St. Manetto, the late General, the fourth of the Founders to receive his summons, was very near his reward. Fra Filippo reached the mountain-friary in time for the last embrace and the last singing together of the *Salve* as St. Manetto happily departed. He died on August 20, the feast of St. Bernard, the sweet singer of Mary's glories into whose mouth Dante many years later was to put the great splendid lyric, "O maiden Mother! daughter of thy Son,"

Vergine madre, figlia del tuo figlio,

which ends the *Paradiso* in a blaze of light and joy. In the presence of large crowds Fra Filippo celebrated the funeral rites, and a day or two later resumed his duties.

For the rest of this year, 1268, there is only one record of him. For the most part he is trudging the roads as usual. On November 6 we find him again in Florence, issuing formal permission to one Arrigo Baldovino, a lay *devoto* or oblate at the Cafaggio friary, to return to his own house. A wealthy man and a generous benefactor to the new Annunziata, Baldovino found the order's daily and nightly austerities too much for him, and Fra Filippo, a doctor himself, had no need of a consultation before sending him home for good. In the February following we encounter the second of the "classic" miracles attributed to Fra Filippo. It took place at Gagliano, on the road from Florence to Bologna.

Andrea del Sarto made a noble fresco of it for the entrance-cloisters of the Santissima Annunziata nearly two and a half centuries later; incidentally placing the scene correctly at Gagliano, whereas another version, confusing the neighbouring *castello* of Montaccianico with Montalcino, places it near Siena. But it was at Gagliano that Fra Filippo, his *socius*, and three other Servite friars, walking together deep in spiritual talk on a day of bitter cold, heard a quavering voice crying from the roadside and saw an elderly leper shivering there, his appalling sores covered by a few rags. None of them possessed a penny, and whatever food they needed on their journey they would have to beg themselves. " 'Silver and gold have I none, brother,' " quoted Fra Filippo from St. Peter, ' "but what I have, I give thee.' " [1] Then, withdrawing a little distance from his companions, and beckoning the leper to

[1] Acts 3: 6.

follow, he quickly divested himself of the woollen tunic
under his habit and over his hair-shirt, handed it to the
leper, bidding him put it on for the love of God ("This
is all I have to give"), and rejoined the others. They had
not gone far before a howl of joy behind them made
them stop, and they saw the late leper bounding towards
them, sound and strong and healed. He tried in vain to
kiss the feet of Filippo, roaring his thanks. "I am a poor
sinner like yourself, brother. Give thanks not to me but
to God and His holy mother, who have cured you, and
go in peace, and tell nobody."

The friars paced on. Before long the whole countryside
had heard about the miracle. In due course it reached the
ears of Cardinal Ubaldini at his family seat of Montaccianico, and doubtless confirmed him in a resolution
already, perhaps, half formed. By the time it came down
to Andrea del Sarto in 1510 the five friars concerned were
wearing white cloaks; a curious example of artistic
whimsy, the master being surrounded by live Servites at
the time. What is held on very good authority to be the
miraculous tunic is still preserved at the Annunziata, with
other Philippine relics; no doubt the beneficiary did not
part with it for nothing. It is a vest of white wool about
a yard long, open at the neck; the surviving sleeve fits
closely at the wrist, and the material, when last examined
before the canonisation process in 1620, was unstained.
With it are preserved one of St. Philip's short black-
leather boots, with the original fastening-hooks (what
survives of a pair of rush-sandals is kept at Rome), and
a portion of a scapular. Personal relics of the saint are
enshrined in two caskets.

2

So we come to an event in the life of Fra Filippo Benizi which, had it happened seven centuries later, would have attracted dazing and deafening publicity from the world's newspaper Press, radio, and television-batteries. "Monk Turns Down Papacy—Vatican Sensation Drama" would probably be the nearest to accuracy one could expect in the way of headlines. The early biographers and the compilers of the canonisation-process take it calmly, and, unfortunately, with no elaboration of an historic happening. As indeed it was. Very few pictures or statues of St. Philip Benizi, and none of modern times, omit the papal tiara at his feet. It is his mark, like the raven of St. Benedict and the roses of St. Thérèse of Lisieux. For his feast-day the Roman Breviary gives the briefest matter-of-fact account:

> Miracles having spread his fame far and wide, certain cardinals assembled at Viterbo to elect a successor to Clement IV, lately deceased, turned their thoughts to Philip, of whose almost celestial prudence they were aware. Discovering this, the man of God fled forthwith to Montamiata to escape the burden of the pastoral office, and Gregory X was elected Pontifex Maximus instead.

It was during a return-visit to Viterbo that Fra Filippo first learned what certain of the Sacred College had in contemplation concerning him. Since the death of Clement IV in that city on November 29, 1268, the assembled cardinals found themselves unable to decide on a successor.[1] Even threats by the irritated citizens of

---

[1] At this period candidature for the Holy See was not confined to members of the Sacred College.

Viterbo in the person of their chief magistrate, or
Podestà, and duly carried out, to reduce them to short
rations, lock them up, and remove the roof of the council-
chamber of the papal palace had no effect. Not till September 1, 1271, was Gregory X elected, and then only by
a chosen committee of six.

It may have been from his fellow-Florentine Cardinal
Ottaviano degl'Ubaldini that Fra Filippo, to his dismay,
learned early in 1269 that his candidature for the tiara was
not only accepted but highly approved by the only strong
group in the Sacred College, the initial move having been
due to Cardinal Fieschi, Protector of the Servite Order in
Rome. Viterbo would be full of gossip and Florence, one
may presume, full of hurraying excitement when the news
got there. The local Guelfs would be in high feather.
Meanwhile at Viterbo Fra Filippo, in a state amounting
to panic, was pleading with Cardinal Fieschi to stop the
proceedings.

His anguished appeals made little or no impression,
Cardinal Fieschi apparently having the answer to every
objection the friar before him could raise. Unworthy of
such an honour? *Va bene*—who is not? Rejecting it
humbly but firmly, heart and soul? *Va bene* again—but
suppose acceptance were the will of God? The Cardinal
must nevertheless have opened his eyes wide on hearing
a remarkable utterance from the suppliant at his feet.

"What's that again?"

"My lord, it is for yourself, not such as I, that the supreme dignity is reserved."

"For me?"

"For you, my lord. By divine Providence you will be
raised to the Chair of St. Peter, though you will not
occupy it long."

And so in fact it happened seven years later. In 1267 Cardinal Ottabuono Fieschi succeeded Innocent V under the title of Adrian V, to die six weeks later and to earn the distinction, still later, of being the only Pope whom Dante meets in Purgatory. It is on the Fifth Terrace, among those being purged of avarice—the old Dantean theme-song, covering the Papacy at large.

After this alarmingly inconclusive audience Fra Filippo realised that his implorations would have no effect at all. On the following night he left Viterbo, secretly, late, and hastily, in the company of Fra Lottaringo and Fra Vittore, taking the direction of Siena and vanishing eventually in wild country some forty-five miles south, near the village of Campiglia, where the peak of Montamiata rises from thick woods and rocky fastnesses. Here, he informed his *socius*, he intended to remain in seclusion till there was no further danger to be apprehended from Viterbo. Meanwhile he accorded Fra Lottaringo full powers to administer the order in his absence, desiring him to postpone the next general chapter till June 24, St. John Baptist; to preside over which Fra Filippo promised to return.

A word on one aspect of this historic incident may be added.

Though there is ample testimony to "the great refusal", modern Italian—and Catholic—scholarship has raised a query about the year of its happening. It is pointed out that in 1268 St. Philip Benizi was only 35 years old and a religious of only fifteen years' standing. The year 1280, after the death of Nicolas III, has been suggested as more likely, the flight to Montamiata notwithstanding. But one may reflect that in 1268 the circumstances were desperate. The cardinals assembled at Viterbo were at a stand, having discussed every possible candidate for the tiara and come to no agreement. Here at hand was an Italian religious of acknowledged and pre-eminent sanctity, proven ability to govern and organise, and diplomatic gifts, with a couple of well-attested miracles attaching to his reputation already. As for St. Philip's age, a man of thirty-five is normally in full maturity and exercise of all his faculties, and it might be possible to discover a precedent or two on this score among the hundred and eighty Popes who had reigned so far, the first fifty especially. Then again there was the political question. Though the late Emperor Frederic II had ceased to vex and assail the Holy See eighteen years previously, his Ghibellines were still a noisy menace all over Italy. A Florentine of good Guelf stock would thus have extra qualifications.

Considering all these things, objections on the score of St. Philip's age seem not insuperable, and as the year 1268 satisfies every other condition it is here accepted, with all deference to authorities more worthy of attention.[1]

3.

Near the grotto on Montamiata which St. Philip found an oasis of solitude (to quote an early biographer, Tavanti) for "the refreshment of a soul parched by the heat and dust of the exterior life", are some pools formed by sulphurated water falling from the rocks and called to this day Bagni San Filippo. A tradition attributing their origin to an act of gratitude by the saint for local kindness during the time of his retreat in this rugged place makes him strike the rocks with his staff. The water gushing

___

[1] The current edition of the *Enciclopedia Italiana* accepts the year 1268 likewise. (Art. "Filippo Benizi, Santo".)

therefrom has certainly proved medicinal for centuries. A similar tradition attaches to the Grotto of St. Philip, a similar fount on Monte Senario, where water miraculously burst from the rock at the prayer of the saint.

Amid the rocks and chestnut-woods of five-hundred-and-eighty-foot-high Montamiata, now crowned by a tall iron cross, Fra Filippo lived for nearly four months, repeating all the devotional austerities of his retreat on Monte Senario. With Fra Vittore's help he turned two of its many grottos into a rough chapel and a rougher cell. A nearby spring supplied his drink. Fresh herbs and—some time later, when to his dismay neighbouring villages discovered his presence—a little coarse bread were sufficient food. A magnificent panorama lay spread at his feet by day; a magnificently starry sky glittered over him at night; it is possible that one so absorbed with Heaven saw very little of either. The splendour of daily Mass at dawn celebrated in a cave on the humblest of makeshift altars, before a rough wooden crucifix carved by himself, must have transcended anything earth had to offer. Visitors became frequent before long. Quitting a celestial company, Fra Filippo received them with his invariably humble courtesy and sped them with good counsel. Towards the middle of June he began reluctant preparations to descend into the world of men again, and on Saturday, June 22, he arrived, as promised, at Cafaggio to preside over the chapter-general, radiating and receiving the warmest affection as usual.

The chapter opened on Monday, June 24. Before it closed Fra Filippo had introduced a little more necessary machinery into the order. At his suggestion the assembled friars unanimously decreed the inauguration of provincial chapters, any proposals made at which four provincial definitors would consider and, if necessary, approve for inclusion in the Constitutions. The chapter also received a surprise. Fra Filippo announced his immediate intention of taking the road to Germany. Complaints were being received from some of the young Servite communities beyond the Alps that they had no contact with head-quarters and their generals never visited them. So far neglect of this sort had been inevitable, the first four generals of the order being men too advanced in age to face the hardships of foreign travel, which in this age were redoubtable. A vigorous general of thirty-six was now to remedy all this; during his absence the order would be administered by Fra Lottaringo. The chapter received Fra Filippo's resolution, it is recorded, with mingled pain at the prospect of a long absence and rejoicing over the beginnings of a new apostolate.

It is perhaps advisable to pause a moment here, while St. Philip is preparing for the road to Germany, to con-sider a somewhat vexing question. Will the forthcoming journey include a visit to France? St. Philip's first dozen biographers have no doubt of it, and the cautious and dependable Fra Alessio Rossi thinks it probable. There is no "hard" documentary evidence, and unfortunately no records survive of thirteenth-century Servite foundations in France. The existence of a house founded by St. Manetto in the Sorbonne quarter of Paris is deducible from contemporary references to Servite students attend-ing the University. Otherwise not even the sites are known. On the whole, perhaps, one might assume with-out offence that St. Philip's journey at this time included France. A biographer of 1516, Fra Cosimo Rucellai, O.S.M., is categorical. "The grace of God going with him, he reached the confines of Italy and entered France by way of Piedmont"—Rucellai's authority is an early Latin MS. preserved at Todi and published in Florence in the 1870's. Amid this fog of uncertainty one fact at least glimmers like a will o' the wisp. Fra Filippo actually left Italy by the Mont Cenis pass, which is the way to France. The remainder of the journey is therefore feasible enough.

Leaving it at that, we return to Florence and the late July of 1269. Attended by the inseparable Fra Vittore and by two of the three elderly survivors of the founding Fathers, Ugo and Sosthenes, the General made for Bologna, where they stayed till August 2. On that day, in the fiery glare of an Italian summer afternoon, they left for the Lombard plain. It is not difficult to picture them trudging very slowly along the dusty highroad in their black woollen habits, shouldering their sacks. An hour or so after leaving Bologna they reached the site of a considerable portent, to which there is sufficient testimony.

At a point of the road near Castroleone, about five miles out of Bologna, a large solitary tree standing in the baking fields a little distance off the highroad offered the only shade for miles. A knot of figures could be seen already under its branches. In compassion for his two elders, now lagging and weary, Fra Filippo turned off the road for a rest. As they approached the tree they were welcomed by raucous laughter and rude japes, and perceived that the group was composed of soldiers and women of the lowest type, possibly drunk. The roughest company was unlikely to daunt a medieval friar, who was well used to it, but this collection proved even worse than the tavern-company which waylays Glutton in *Piers Plowman* on his way to confession:

Sisse the sempstress sat on the bench,
Watte the warrener and his wife, drunk,
Tom the tinker and two of his knaves,
Hick the hackneyman and Hugh the needler,
An hayward and an heremyte, the hangman of Tyburn,
Darew the dyker with a dozen hirelots
Of porters and of pickpurses and bald tooth-drawers,
A rybibour and a ratcatcher, a raker and his knave ...

Under a fusillade of obscenities and blasphemous
raillery Fra Filippo spoke up, rebuking the offenders,
firmly but without heat, in the name of Christ and His
mother, and bidding them amend their language for their
souls' sake. They received the reproof with viler insults
and louder and uglier blasphemies, the women doubtless
being far more fluent than the men. As they bellowed and
screamed and laughed a premonition came to St. Philip.
"My dear brethren," he said, facing them during a pause
with tears in his eyes, "there are some of you here who,
unless they repent, are due to die this very day. Almighty
God is very kind and pitiful. Turn you to Him and He
will have mercy on you—He has sent me even now to
call on you for this. Be certain that if you turn to Him He
will forgive, but if you refuse you may well tremble. His
bow is bent, His arrows are sharp, the weapons of death
are ready. Give up this vicious life and trust in His mercy
who does not desire the death of a sinner, but rather that
he may turn from his wickedness and live."

The words in their quiet earnestness had some effect.
The majority sobered down in shame, as the typical
medieval ruffian was always liable to do when so addressed; but a blackguard minority turned angry, belch-
ing horrid blasphemy and menacing the friar with violent

consequences if he did not shut his mouth and go. Fra
Filippo continued unmoved to plead with them. "Unless
you repent and do penance", he assured them, "the fire
of God's wrath will most surely fall on you this very
day." After renewed profanity and threats he gave up.
"Come, brethren," he said sadly to his three companions
and to those of the late scoffers who had listened to him.
"We had better go, and quickly. I see God's wrath about
to fall on these unhappy creatures."

Leading the way back to the road, and followed by
most of his late assailants, he turned at a distance and made
a final plea to the others. "If I have offended you, my
brothers, forgive me. But I implore you not to delay
repentance, or soon—very soon now—you will feel the
scourge of God's anger."

As he ended, amid jeers, the brassy sky turned black
overhead and a violent thunderstorm broke in torrents of
rain. Before the four friars and a now agitated cluster of
soldiers and women reached the highway they turned to
see the big tree and those remaining under it enveloped
suddenly in smoke and flame. When this cleared, a
moment later, nothing was visible but a heap of ashes.
Falling on their knees, Fra Filippo and his three brethren
prayed loud and long as the storm passed for the souls of
the dead, who might by God's mercy have had time to
make an act of contrition. And at length, having taken
leave of their trembling fellows and received their
promises to amend their lives henceforth, the General and
his brethren resumed their journey in the heat.

Such was the Judgment of Castroleone; less a miracle,
remarks Fra Luigi Pazzaglia, than a clairvoyance. A chapel
on the site, built by the Servites of Bologna at the beginning of the eighteenth century, perpetuates the memory

of an event attested by three saints and half a dozen or more other eye-witnesses, and therefore to be adjudged sufficiently authentic. Andrea del Sarto's fresco in the cloisters of the Annunziata illustrates it superbly.

One by one the General visited the Servite priories of the Lombard province. How many had been already founded is not recorded. There was certainly a priory in Milan; the priory at Asti was founded in 1263, and the other three noted in a survey of 1300—Parma, Reggio Emilia, and Alessandria—may have existed in 1269 as well. In the priory at Tortona, a room known as "St. Philip's cell" was shown down to nearly the end of the eighteenth century.

Leaving Tortona, they came by way of Alessandria and Asti, and possibly Turin, to the Mont Cenis pass, toiling up its ascending spirals and over and down again on the French side. We who rush up and down the Mont Cenis nowadays so swiftly and so easily on wheels may profitably pause to recollect that these four or five friars, two of them advanced in years, were performing the first long instalment of a journey of many hundreds of miles made on foot, in sandals, with no aid but a staff, no food except what the charitable gave them, no drink but water from some wayside spring or brook, no lenitive for sore or bleeding feet but what adjacent woods provided, no first-aid in accidents, no protection from rain, snow, intense heat, or biting cold but their habits, dry or soaked, no comfort at the day's end but a truss of straw in some barn or outbuilding, or, if they were fortunate, a cell in some religious house on the road. Considering these things, we may feel we have little to boast of in the way of stamina. On the other hand it is true that Fra Filippo and his companions fitted into the thirteenth-century landscape, so to speak, far more than they would do into a modern one. The highroads of medieval Europe were well used to pilgrims and mendicants for the love of God, charity was not yet the affair of the State, the Faith was a universal language, and travel was open to all. On the whole, and all spiritual considerations apart, those four trudging, limping, or hobbling figures may be envied by the beneficiaries of Progress as they fade from our sight.

Which direction they took on touching French soil can only, as we have already seen, be conjectured. They must have got as far into Savoy as Modane or St. Jean-de-Maurienne, the first two villages under the mountains. In the church of St. Jean-de-Maurienne which is now the smallest of French cathedrals, Fra Filippo may have said a Mass before going on. They may then have turned south, as some of the early biographers assert in pages glowing with accounts of St. Philip's progress, his preaching of the Servite message on the roadside and in villages, the flocking of postulants, carefully weeded out, the foundation of new French houses, the granting of the black scapular of the Dolours[1] to aspirants compelled to live in the world. It is stated that the journey of some two thousand miles, so far, culminated in a brief visit to Paris, and that before leaving France the General appointed Fra Sosthenes Vicar-General of the new province and left him behind. Here at any rate we find some firm ground. Fra Sosthenes ruled the French Province for the next six years, won the esteem of the Crown, and enabled the Servite priory in Paris founded by St. Manetto to acquire a standing in the University under the generalship of Fra Lottaringo, St. Philip's immediate successor.

[1] To be distinguished from the Confraternity scapular, a later development.

4.

Of Fra Filippo's journey into Germany in this year 1271 there is no doubt. Pontifical letters of protection and other documents cited in the *Monumenta Ordinis Servorum Sanctae Mariae* show that there were several Servite houses in Germany at this time, not yet organised into a Province, and probably ruled (thinks Fr. Rossi) by a vicar-general. As with other houses beyond the Alps, they were feeling cut off from Servite circulation. Fra Filippo was the first of five generals to be able to visit them in person.

At St. Philip's death, according to a MS. preserved at Arezzo, there were fourteen houses of the order in Germany; four in Saxony, two in Bavaria, the others in Austria, Thuringia, Wurtemburg, Anhalt, and Cassel. Fra Filippo himself founded, now or later, houses at Frankfort, Cracow, and Emden. The order had been established in Germany round about 1255, five years after the Emperor Fredric II's death ended his long conflict with the Holy See and landed him, in so far as Dante was empowered to decide Frederic's eternal destiny, in the sixth circle of Hell with the arch-heretics, his penitent end and absolution notwithstanding. In the year of the Emperor's death the then Servite General, St. Bonfiglio, was granted a licence from Rome to absolve those of Frederic's partisans, excommunicate like himself, who wished to take the Servite habit; a concession applying to Italians and Germans equally. In both countries many of the late Emperor's men availed themselves of this. In both a hard core of hostility to the Holy See survived. With a few ugly current heresies, this goes to make the obverse side of the most glorious century in European history, the age of the cathedrals, the guilds, and the *Summa*.

Having crossed the Rhine Fra Filippo and his companions, Fra Ugo, Fra Vittore, and two or three other friars unnamed, at length entered what the old chroniclers describe with their usual exasperating vagueness as a vast and gloomy forest; undoubtedly, agree later annotators, the Black Forest, celebrated in all German folklore as a realm of sombre terrors. Its native population of demons, kobolds, goblins, and witches would hold no menace for servants of Mary armed with a chaplet apiece—a spiritual weapon with which, one feels, Hansel and Gretel would have been able to do useful work had their creator thought of it. Bears, wolves, and brigands were a more material source of discomfort to the contemporary traveller. None of these fauna loomed in the Servites' path, but a mishap almost as disastrous befell Fra Filippo and his brethren. Having no guide, they lost their way. Towards sunset on their first day's journey the friars found themselves in a trackless maze of huge trees and impenetrable undergrowth, with no sign of human existence anywhere and, of course, no hope of food or drink. It was mid-July and the heat was intense. Two days later, their hunger and thirst being now intolerable, they were still wandering. By this time one of the brethren—unnamed, but almost certainly Fra Ugo—could drag himself no further. As they gazed haggardly at each other, as Fra Filippo resumed praying aloud with greater intensity, they heard a shout. Some distance away a couple of woodmen were beckoning them from the door of a hut in a clearing which they had not hitherto observed. Before they could reach the hut the woodmen had vanished. The friars entered the hut, which was empty. On a table lay a loaf of good bread apiece, with a pitcher of clear cold water nearby.

With grateful thanks to God and Our Lady they restored themselves and continued their way along a track which revealed itself near the hut. Before long they emerged on the highroad. Without doubt their rescuers, whom they saw no more, were from Heaven. They continued their journey with great happiness.

From here their itinerary, covering Franconia, Friesland, and Saxony, is impossible to trace. We know, however, that they split into pairs and, having sufficient German, traversed the countryside in apostolic-wise, preaching the Dolours of Mary to all who would listen. The natives received them responsively, though they seem to have encountered the customary hostility from those pre-Lutheran enemies of the Faith whose idol and exemplar had been Frederic II in his prime. The records speak of occasional insults and threats, at once a permitted trial and a demonstration of the gift of free-will to the meanest of God's creatures. We catch up with Fra Filippo and his brethren at last in the great proud commercial babel of Frankfort-on-the-Main. Here Fra Filippo was able to discover a pearl of great price. In this city of merchants and money-changers—Frankfort had also, of course, a sufficiency of churches and religious houses—was a young man of great piety known to the chroniclers as Blessed Johann of Frankfort. Directed by Our Lady in a dream to seek out "Father Philip, an Italian religious in a black habit, now preaching in this city", he hastened to wait on the foreign friars, begging Fra Filippo to admit him into their order. It was Fra Filippo's normal custom to put postulants through preliminary tests of considerable severity, doubtless with a medical examination thrown in, but young Johann, an obviously ideal candidate, with no family ties, was judged suitable to receive the novice's habit almost immediately. His quality may be judged by the fact that after only eight years in the order he was elected Vicar-General for Germany by a chapter-general at Orvieto. He died in Frankfort in 1345. His tomb was destroyed by the Lutherans in the sixteenth century.

Fra Filippo stayed in Germany on this occasion for at least six months, evangelising extensively. He is said during this time to have penetrated as far as Emden to the north and Cracow in Poland, where he founded a house, to the east. The language difficulty seems to have been very slight. He had learned a little German, apparently, at the University of Paris, and more from German friars of the order since his arrival. One of his early biographers, Poccianti, says that he had a natural gift of tongues and could make himself understood however barbarous the local dialect. It is a not unusual gift in God's servants in any age.

The time came for his return to Florence, whence he had received several imploring messages. Misgivings connected with the offer of the tiara being now at an end, Fra Filippo judged that his mission abroad was, for the time, concluded. Having called a provincial chapter and nominated Fra Ugo as Vicar-General for Germany, he began the homeward journey, stopping at Servite priories on the way, and returned to France, arriving in Paris round about September, 1271.

It was apparently a brief and hurried visit. Fra Filippo's object was to get an audience of Louis IX and to ensure royal protection for the order in France. The Paris house, under Fra Sosthenes, was now firmly established and in close contact with the University. Later in the century the Servites would begin to make a figure in the Sorbonne schools. They had not done so before because seeking academic distinction had seemed to conflict with the humility on which the order rests. But its lack of learned men was being made a reproach. In the succeeding centuries it was to provide a sufficiency of theologians, scholars, artists, and scientists.

Meanwhile Louis IX received Fra Filippo cordially and assured him of protection. This fine, strong, just Capet, himself a saint, had an affectionate esteem for the mendicant orders which he did not invariably extend towards a French hierarchy inclined, in his view, to encroach on state preserves and excommunicate his lieges, in gross or detail, on the slightest provocation. As a member of the Franciscan Third Order St. Louis would especially approve Servite poverty, humility, and that special devotion to Our Lady which he shared. Taking leave of him with a light heart, Fra Filippo convoked a provincial chapter to confirm Fra Sosthenes as Vicar-General. The end of his allocution has been preserved in essence:

Let us then serve this divine Master and His blessed mother not in the vanity of our minds but in newness of spirit, even as the Prophet would have us do when he says in the psalm: "Sing ye to the Lord a new canticle". Obey your superiors and be faithful to that which you have promised.

In order that you may perform all these duties, and diligently instruct others therein, I again give you for your father and appoint as my Vicar-General in France the Reverend Father Sosthenes of Florence. As he was one of the founders of our order, so will he be its preserver and propagator in the province. Obey him humbly, as being a minister of Christ Jesus and a devout servant of His blessed mother, and walk in his footsteps, as he strives to walk in those of our Lord and Redeemer, whom I beseech to bless us and grant us all spiritual good and to help us now and always. May He be pleased also to be with me in this journey.

And Fra Filippo took leave of them, and accompanied by the faithful Fra Vittore, Fra Walther from Germany, and Fra Giovanni of Florence, began the trudge south, entering Switzerland at Lausanne, preaching there with recorded success, crossing the Great St. Bernard, coming down to Aosta far below, and so home.

Lutheran violence was to wipe out the German Servite Province almost entirely in the sixteenth century. It was not revived till 1954. In France the order was to suffer many vicissitudes. During that unhappy visitation called the Great Schism of the West, the French Servites not only sided, like the rest of France, with the antipope Clement VII, Robert of Geneva, whereas in every other country the order took the side of the *de jure* Urban VI, but joined themselves afterwards to the now-extinct order called the "Billettes", or Hospitallers of the Charity of Our Lady, who likewise followed St. Augustine's rule.[1] Though subsequent attempts to reclaim them for the Servite obedience failed, five regular priories of the order were founded from Italy in the south of France in the sixteenth and seventeenth centuries. A plague-epidemic in the eighteenth decimated most of these communities. The Jansenists and the *philosophes* completed the work. Soon after the outbreak of the Revolution the order in France was extinct, being revived there only a few years ago. Among the reasons for failure to take permanent

---

[1] They enjoyed the curious distinction, in the seventeenth century, of having inspired Molière's only known piece of devotional verse—eight lines.

root in France and Germany one of the order's modern historians, Fr. Peregrine Soulier of the English Province, very frankly includes lack of zeal in some of St. Philip's successors in the generalate. "Very few of their number followed his example by visiting those countries (the Transalpine Provinces, as they were called in Italy) in person. In some cases, no doubt, they were unavoidably prevented. In others, their reign of office was not of sufficient length to enable them to carry out any idea of the kind. Still, several who might have so acted failed to act, and the religious in France and Germany more than once complained of this neglect ... Hence, little by little, the spirit of the Order became relaxed. Thanks be to God, such is no longer the case."[1]

Thus to the material benefits brought about by steam, electricity and petrol may be added not a few of a kind which would have surprised, and in some cases dismayed, the benefactors responsible.

5.

On the eve of quitting Germany Fra Filippo despatched a friar to Florence with a message for Fra Lottaringo, his *locum tenens*. He was to summon all concerned to a chapter-general to be held at Borgo San Sepolchro, now called Sansepolchro, in the Marche, some sixty miles south of Florence.

Since German spite blew up the ancient Torre di Berta on the main piazza in 1944 not much of St. Philip's time survives in this agreeable little town except the Duomo; its enduring pride and joy, the stupendous Resurrection fresco by Sansepolchro's greatest son, Piero della Fran-

[1] *Life of Saint Philip Benizi*. London, 1886.

cesca, was yet to come. The town was chosen for the chapter-general of April 1272 on account of a projected new Servite church and priory to replace one founded by Fra Sosthenes in 1255 some distance from the town. At the conclusion of the chapter the first stone was duly laid by St. Philip in the presence of all the citizens. Unfortunately the site, just outside the walls, was soon made uninhabitable for the Servites of Sansepolchro owing to constant raids by outlaws and bad characters expelled from the town, and in 1294 a third priory, predecessor of the present one, was built inside the walls.

Fra Filippo had reached Florence near the end of October, 1271, having stopped on the way to inspect a new priory at Mandello, near Milan, and spent a few days in retreat on Monte Senario. At the chapter-general he again attempted to resign the generalship. Once more his petition was lovingly and firmly rejected. Once more he set out on a visitation, this time of the priories of Tuscany and Umbria. Once more crowds flocked everywhere to hear him preach. Once more, this time at Siena, he received an outstanding new recruit into the order; a young aristocrat of angelic goodness to whom, under the name of Blessed Giovacchino of Siena, his fellow-citizens still pay devotion. He belonged to the Piccolomini family, which has given the Church two popes, one of whom, the brilliant humanist and diplomat Pius II, Aeneas Sylvius, bequeathed to posterity those written impressions of fifteenth-century Scotland which so resemble those of an indulgent *grand seigneur* surveying the aboriginals of Tierra del Fuego. The clothing of young Giovacchino Chiaramonte-Piccolomini with the Servite habit had a slightly more eventful prelude than most, since his very devout parents, unable to contemplate their separation, very nearly brought off a kidnapping. As a friar he has another distinction. Wrung by the paroxysms of an epileptic in hospital at Arezzo, he implored Our Lord to allow him to take the poor man's malady on himself. His petition was immediately granted. The epileptic rose up cured, and from that day to his death Blessed Giovacchino was a victim of the "falling sickness", with all the suffering that implies. A truly heroic character, whose dying-bed in many ways recalls that of Huysmans' heroine, Blessed Lydwine of Schiedam. It is claimed in Siena, where the body of the *beatus* lies under the high altar of Santa Maria dei Servi, that many epileptics have been healed by his intercession.

There is not much record of Fra Filippo's activities during most of the year 1272. New priories were projected and built, and others enlarged. Visitations continued. Almsgiving was generous. Early in 1273 Fra Filippo was informed in a letter from Cardinal Ottabuono Fieschi, Protector of the Order, that Gregory X was preparing to set out for the Second Council of Lyons, and that a consultation in Florence beforehand was imperative in Servite interests. An imminent chapter-general at Arezzo prevented Fra Filippo from meeting the cardinal immediately. As soon as the chapter closed he hastened to Florence.

Pope Gregory X was already in the city, having paused on his way to Lyons to attempt, if possible, to pacify the Florentines, who were maiming and murdering one another with tireless energy in the eternal Guelf-Ghibelline quarrel. On July 12 it seemed as if a month's exhortations and diplomacy by Gregory had brought the hotheads to reason. A public reconciliation-ceremony was held. Guelf and Ghibelline formally clasped hands and swore to keep the peace. The Pope's contentment lasted nearly a week. The clubs, swords, and daggers then came out again, and the streets of Florence rang with the old yells, oaths, and steel-clashings, and a weary and indignant Pontiff placed the city under an interdict and left for Mugello, a few miles away, where he stayed for a time as the guest of the Ubaldini family, waiting for the fools of Florence to change their minds.

They did not, being about as open to reason, not to speak of the penalties of the Church, as two sets of furious dogs. When *la rabbia* seized the old-time Florentine populace, as it did very notably during the upheavals of Savonarola's time, it was a serious business. All else apart, the small boys of Florence were international aces at stone-throwing. But the Guelf-Ghibelline affrays of St. Philip's time were not mere proletarian self-expressionism. As already observed, they were aristocratic group-feuds conducted more or less on the Highland pattern. Should the noblemen involved, with their male offspring and relations, grow languid in active hate, which to do them justice was rare, their armed retainers could be relied on to keep up hostilities, insulting and provoking each other whenever they met in the streets and calling up reinforcements with a whistle or a yell. "Do you bite your thumb at us, sir?"—Shakespeare's glimpse of the Montecchi-Capuletti feud in Verona three hundred years later gives us the thirteenth-century Florentine picture on a small scale. Though they can hardly be described as gangsters, as the Compagnacci of Florence under the super-tough Doffo Spini in Savonarola's day certainly could be, neither Guelfs nor Ghibellines gave a brass *soldo* for the Queensberry Rules, and assassination was as normal as any other form of mayhem. It is quite useless for well-groomed Nordic professors in rimless pince-nez to try to understand these men. Their world was young and violent and they were Italians capable of great sins and exquisite sanctity, to neither of which a well-groomed Nordic professor can normally aspire. Meanwhile it may be said in behalf of the Ghibellines of Florence that it was not they who started the fighting again after the "reconciliation" of July, 1273, but their enemies; the Guelfs, the Pope's men, who seem to have cared not a rap for either the Holy Father's appeals or his interdict, which lasted three years.[1]

In the Annals of the Servite Order, revised, corrected, and augmented by the erudite Fra Luigi Garbi of Lucca in 1719 from the edition of Giani a century earlier, it is briefly recorded that during the recent troubles Fra Filippo Benizi had himself striven, in conjunction with the Pope, and after his departure, to bring peace to Florence, but in vain. The hatreds dividing the city were as yet too much for him. We find him next (March 1274) in Siena presiding at a chapter-general, preparatory to starting for Lyons like other heads of orders. On May 7 the Second Oecumenical Council of Lyons, fourteenth of its kind, was opened by Gregory X in the presence of five hundred bishops, Latin and Greek, seventy abbots, about a thousand minor prelates, and twenty ambassadors, including sixteen Tartars. The council is chiefly remarkable for the solemn and, alas, temporary abjuration of the Greek Orthodox schism made before it, in the name of the Emperor Michael VIII Palaeologue of Byzantium, by his chief minister, Giorgios Akropolitis; a move inspired

---

[1] Under such an interdict, normally speaking, marriages could be solemnised and the last Sacraments were given to the dying and Christian burial to the dead. Otherwise there was severe curtailment of Masses, Offices, and all spiritual privileges.

less by religious compunction than by fear of the Turks.[1]
Of more immediate moment to Fra Filippo and to Cardinal Fieschi, Protector of the Servites, was a decree
concerning the religious orders. It has been mentioned in
an earlier page. The operative clause conveyed a threat
to the whole Servite future:

> We wholly forbid and altogether abolish all mend-
> icant orders founded since the aforesaid Council [the
> Fourth Lateran of 1215, forbidding the foundation of
> any new order] which have not received confirmation
> by the Apostolic See.

There was a rider to this. Any mendicant order approved since the Fourth Lateran Council was to receive
no more novices and found no more houses. The case of
non-mendicant orders in the same position was adjourned
for future consideration.

It looked like total suppression of the Order of the
Servants of Mary. Founded since the Fourth Lateran
Council, it had received approbation from two Popes,
Alexander IV and Urban IV, but no official confirmation.
If it could be shown to be not entirely a mendicant order,
a legal point established later, it was only relatively in a
better position, the question of such orders founded since
1215 having been left in abeyance. As soon as possible
Cardinal Fieschi, after consultation with the General,
sought an audience of the Holy Father and presented a
petition from Fra Filippo. Its main plea was that the order
had been founded by Our Lady's express command, and
it recalled many favours and achievements in the spiritual
sphere.[2] The petition was backed by several influential

---

[1] The schism was re-established in 1285 by Andronicus II of Byzantium.
[2] The visions of 1233 and 1240, being "private revelations", were not of
obligatory acceptance by anyone not directly concerned.

delegates to the late Council who had met Fra Filippo and had been impressed by his sanctity. After listening very favourably the Pope gave the order a verbal approbation, *vivae vocis oraculo*, and confirmed its existing privileges. His implication seemed to be that official and definitive recognition would be pronounced when he had examined the matter thoroughly at leisure.

The wished-for document never arrived in Florence. Gregory X died within two years, leaving the Servite Order existent but still lacking final recognition. With this relative satisfaction Fra Filippo left again for Germany, now recovering under Rudolf I of Hapsburg from the anarchy and chaos following the death of Frederic II.

Apart from a visitation of the German Servite priories Fra Filippo had a mission from the Holy See to the new Emperor. Since the deplorable end of the Fourth Crusade (1201-5) in the sack of Byzantium with almost Turkish ruthlessness by the Venetians and the feudal barons who turned a crusade into a business proposition, the Holy Sepulchre had remained in the infidel's hands. At Gregory X's urging the Second Council of Lyons had debated the organising of yet another attempt to free it. The new ruler of the Holy Roman Empire, on being approached by Fra Filippo on this subject, promised to consider the matter as soon as he had settled his numerous troubles in Germany with seditious barons, brawling heretics, and a hostile King of Bohemia. He even took the Cross at Lausanne in October 1275, though unable to go further. Rudolf of Hapsburg was a very different character from his enigmatic predecessor, being a strong ally of the Holy See against French and other troublemakers, and so sterling a Christian that Dante could very nearly forgive him for not taking over Italy. One may recall that Rodolf gets off with a very light rebuke when the poet finds him in Purgatory, seated with other rulers in the Valley of the Princes during the singing of the *Salve Regina* at sunset. "He that sits highest, and has the look of having been heedless of his duty, and does not move his lips with the singing of the rest, was Rudolf the Emperor, who might have healed the wounds that have slain Italy":

> Rodolfo imperador fu, che potea
> sanar le piaghe c'hanno Italia morta ...[1]

The old Dantean obsession, we observe. As happens now and again in the *Divine Comedy*, the politician has conquered the poet. Why the Emperor Rodolf of Hapsburg, having refrained from settling the affairs of Italy, should refrain likewise from joining in the *Salve* with his brother-princes remains one of the many enigmas of the *Commedia*. The Rodolf of actuality had a particular devotion to Our Lady, and is recorded in the Servite Annals and by the contemporary Czech historian Czerwenka to have accepted the scapular of the Dolours from Fra Filippo Benizi during this very visit. His Empress, Anne of Hohemberg, the Bishop of Mainz, and several members of the Imperial Court did the same.

After some months of visitations, preachings, and other pastoral work in the Empire Fra Filippo returned to his native land—how many leagues of weariness, what physical trials may this simple phrase imply!—to be greeted with appeals for help from Bologna, which university city was now excelling itself for noise and tumult.

Like nearly every other Italian city at the beginning of 1276 Bologna was the arena of a dogfight. A running

[1] *Purgatorio*, vii, 94-5.

feud between two great local clans, the Gieremei and the Lambertazzi, arrayed most of the citizenry on one side or the other. Already the Dominicans and Franciscans in the city had tried a score of times to pacify the combatants. Whenever they were successful, the truces were broken next day. St. Philip's co-operation is not recorded in detail, but since the Senate of Bologna within a month or two voted a handsome sum towards the enlargement of the Servite house in that city, with a new dormitory to be built at the public expense, his success may be lawfully deduced. He left Bologna at length for Florence, where the position was now worse than it had been for some time. Since the death of Giovanni Mangiadoro, Bishop of Florence, in December 1274, the see had been vacant, and violent faction-quarrels even over the question of a successor were frequent. Preaching daily to large crowds at the Annunziata Fra Filippo harangued his fellow-citizens, noble, bourgeois, and proletarian, with eloquence and point. If they were incapable of making peace for themselves, he cried one evening, they might at least unite in praying the Holy See to give Florence a bishop capable of settling their foolish and murderous quarrels.

This seems to have penetrated. As the preacher continued a buzz went round the crowd. The Annals preserve the gist of it. Vivacious Tuscan gestures and flashing dark eyes may be easily supplied in imagination.

"Himself—who else?"
"A fellow-citizen."
"His family—everybody knows it!"
"Holy and prudent."
"Didn't they try to make him Pope not so long ago?"

"Fra Filippo ..."

"Why not he, instead of some bishop we'd know nothing about?"

"Fra Filippo ..."

A cry was heard. Other voices took it up amid a forest of gesticulating arms.

"Filippo! Fra Filippo for our bishop!"

At which, bringing his discourse to an abrupt end, the Prior-General hastily descended the pulpit steps, clove his way through to the sacristy, and quitted Florence then and there for some refuge unknown, and probably Monte Senario, to emerge a week or two later at Pistoia, in time for the chapter-general which opened there on May 24.[1]

In Pistoia the citizens were brawling politically and socially as elsewhere—Guelf against Ghibelline, Canci-elleri against Panciatichi. In Pistoia likewise the generosity of the municipality and private citizens towards the religious orders, and the mendicants in particular, in the matter of alms for building and endowment, demonstrates that typically medieval blend of ungovernable passions and unstinted charity which is so baffling to a modern world. Guelf and Ghibelline, having listened to the same Mass and sermon and given alms in the same dish, would whip out their swords again outside the church door and resume the fight. In his exhortations from the pulpit Fra Filippo minced no words, judging by what fragments are preserved by Poccianti and others. The city, like Florence and others, is an accursed and wretched Babylon and its citizens are men of blood,

---

[1] The Florentines did not get a new bishop till 1286, the year after St. Philip's death.

creatures with neither sense nor reason, sacrificing human lives and souls to the Evil One their idol; calling on the Lord only in blasphemy, inviting His terrible judgment. Yet if they will but seek peace, the God of Peace will forgive and be with them all.

Meanwhile we, servants of the Most Blessed Virgin, implore her to obtain for you from Almighty God the blessings of peace, unity, and concord. If we forget you, brethren, let our right hand be forgotten, let our tongues cleave to our jaws. Suffer yourselves then to be persuaded when we entreat you to lay aside your dissensions ...

His words had considerable effect. Many conversions are spoken of by the early chroniclers; many scenes of reconciliation between enemies, many returns to the practice of religion, not a few recruits to the Servants of Mary. Among these in Pistoia was a leading Ghibelline bravo named Vanni Buonaccurso, noted for impiety, ferocity, and bloodlust. Having heard a sermon by St. Philip, he followed him afterwards into the priory and fell on his knees, saying that God's word had pierced his heart and begging to be heard in confession. Soon afterwards he was admitted into the noviciate of the Servants of Mary. He turned out as passionate in good work as he had been in evildoing. The cultus of Blessed Bonaventure of Pistoia was approved in 1828.

V

SUNSHINE AND STORM

I.

ON January 21, 1276, eleven days after the death of Gregory X, a new Pope ascended the throne. Pierre de Tarantaise, who took the name of Innocent V, was an exemplary French Dominican and a stickler for *la forme*. He had not been Pope for many weeks before Fra Filippo Benizi received a communication from Cardinal Fieschi, Protector of the Order. It informed him that in the opinion of the Holy Father the twenty-third decree of the Second Council of Lyons, now operative, covered the Order of the Servants of Mary. Fra Filippo was accordingly summoned to Rome for formal notification that no more novices were to be admitted to the order, that no more Servite priories were to be opened, that all the order's property was to be considered as transferred to the Holy See and inalienable under pain of excommunication, and finally, that no Servite in Holy Orders could henceforth hear the confessions of the laity or give them burial. In a word, the order was earmarked for extinction.

The blow was unexpected and a grievous one, not only to Fra Filippo but to all the superiors of neighbouring priories, whom he hastily summoned to Monte Senario to hear the news. After taking all measures with Fra Lottaringo to ward off any attack from hostile prelates or others who might have heard of the papal decision and might seek to take early advantage of it, Fra Filippo left for Rome. During this period of anxiety he had been consoled and strengthened, according to a firm tradition, by a vision of Our Lady assuring him that no harm should come to the order, and directing the daily recital in every priory of five psalms and antiphons beginning with the letters M, A, R, I, A in succession. This devotion has flourished ever since.

Fra Filippo had barely begun his journey when the news arrived of Innocent V's death on June 22. He pressed on, reaching Rome in the second week of July to learn that Innocent's successor, Adrian V, was his and the order's old friend Cardinal Ottobuono Fieschi, their late protector. Some biographers have called this a surprise, which, seeing that St. Philip is said seven years previously to have prophesied Fieschi's elevation, it may not have been. Unfortunately both parts of the prophecy were fulfilled. Adrian V was already a sick man. Within six weeks he was dead, having been neither consecrated—he was a cardinal deacon—nor crowned. His successor, "Petrus Hispanus", a Portuguese scholar taking the title of John XXI, was as yet unknown outside the Schools.

Fresh anxieties came crowding on the General immediately. The Servite Order did not lack unfriendly and even hostile critics, in Rome and elsewhere, who considered it an upstart excrescence on the tree of the Regulars and would be glad to see it suppressed. Rumours spread that the order was looked on with a chilly eye at the Vatican and was in domestic difficulties in any case. This latter story had grounds to some extent. A few of the weaker brethren, judging their order to be doomed, had already begun sowing discord and transferring themselves to others approved by the Council of Lyons. But the majority of Servites stood firm and hopeful, looking to God, Our Lady of Sorrows, and their general, himself calm, prudent, and alert to remind all enemies that the Holy See had not yet pronounced final sentence. He had already secured the order a strong new ally in the person of Cardinal Giovanni Orsini, of the great Roman family. Orsini had had a considerable share in the election of John XXI, and the fact that the new Pope had qualified in medicine at the University of Paris was, perhaps, not unfavourable news to Fra Filippo either. But John XXI was a logician likewise—his *Compendium of Logic* was a textbook for three hundred years—and it looked at first as if any attempt to upset Innocent V's ruling would be a waste of time.

However, John XXI duly accepted a petition from Fra Filippo, presented with warm recommendations by Cardinal Orsini, and after giving it consideration passed it on to some of the Consistory lawyers for a report. Meanwhile Fra Filippo himself took legal opinion, a far from inexpensive luxury then as now, putting the Servite case to several jurists of the Curia and asking for a judgment in writing. They agreed that the Servite Order was not on the list for extinction under the decree of the Second Council of Lyons, since technically speaking it was not a mendicant order "within the meaning of the Act". The operative part of this opinion is as follows:

Taking into consideration that your order is founded on the Rule of the Blessed Augustine and that neither your vows nor the constitutions of your order forbid you to hold real or personal property, both of which are possessed by some of your houses; considering also that the Apostolic See has conferred on you the power of holding chapters-general and of electing a prior-general, our opinion is that your order does not seem to us to fall under the law of suppression decreed by the said constitution. And in saying this, we speak according to our conscience, always under submission to any interpretation and declaration which the Holy See may make hereafter.[1]

This turned out to be the view of John XXI's lawyers equally. His decision therefore was that matters should go on for the present as they were, the order continuing to enjoy all its rights and privileges, until the Holy See could pronounce final judgment. In other words, the Servites were placed on the same footing as the Carmelites and the Hermits of St. Augustine; officially approved though not yet officially confirmed, and with every prospect of receiving this and other favours in due course.

This welcome news was duly announced by Fra Filippo to a chapter-general convened at Montepulciano on May 16, and undoubtedly celebrated by many lay adherents of the Servites in and around that charming steep little town in bumpers of the *vino nobile* for which Montepulciano is traditionally celebrated. The assembly of the chapter was itself an answer to those who assumed the Order of Servants of Mary to be under sentence of death. The public preaching of Fra Filippo and other friars during its session was another demonstration of legality. But just as the sky seemed to have cleared, fresh thunderclouds covered it. While the chapter-general was still celebrating the order's reprieve an unforeseen accident threw it once more into alarm and dismay. The scaffolding of a new library being built on to the Papal palace at Viterbo

[1] *Annals*, i, 122.

collapsed as John XXI was inspecting it, and on May 20 he died of his injuries. Who was to guess what the next Pope might do?

For the next six months Fra Filippo Benizi strove valiantly to dispel the fears and depressions of his many hundreds of brethren, himself keeping a cheerful heart and leaving all things to the will of God and the intercession of Our Lady. And once again the sky cleared. On November 25, 1277, Cardinal Giovanni Orsini, Protector of the Servite Order, was elected Pope, taking the name of Nicolas III. Had he but known it, a disturbing destiny was to be reserved for him by one of his new Florentine subjects, at this moment a boy of twelve; namely that of being sentenced to burn for ever in the third *bolgia* of Hell with his fellow-Pope Boniface VIII, "writhing in torment more than any other of his fellows, licked by a redder flame".[1] Such a blasting sentence on a staunch friend to the Servite Order, continuously esteemed by St. Philip Benizi, represents Dante in his most violent red-rag mood, charging head down like a Miura bull at the papal fiscal system ("avarice") and enveloping Nicolas III in a general roar of "Simony!" But the medieval Holy See's system of exacting its dues was none of Nicolas' devising, and nepotism, or the Family Spirit, must be distinguished from simony, or traffic in spiritualities, of which the Middle Ages were at times certainly not innocent. Ecclesiastical nepotism in reasonable degree, if the motives and the recipients be worthy, is no crime— quite often a Pope's relatives might be the best men available—though it was opposed on principle by St. Bernard and St. Bonaventure, condemned by half a dozen or more late-medieval and Renaissance Popes, and finally

[1] *Inferno*, xix, 32-120.

abolished by a Bull of Innocent XII in 1692. Fra Filippo, who did not move in Vatican circles, was preoccupied with greater matters than the ethics of lavishing important offices *en famille*. Of such a procedure, if he ever heard of it, he would, knowing what he did of Nicolas III, assume that there could be no harm done. The new Pope's character was sufficient to warrant unbrokenly cordial relations, and what was good enough for a saint of Philip's quality may be taken as good enough for anybody. One of Nicholas III's first acts after coronation was to hand over his protectorship of the Servites to an ideal successor, his nephew Latino Malebranca; a Dominican scholar-diplomat of unquestioned integrity, one of three new Orsini cardinals created, as Nicolas III proclaimed, to offset "alien influences" in the Curia.

Thus at long last ended, or seemed to end, a dreary sequence of disappointments, trials, vexations, and even persecutions, including several attempts to prevent Fra Filippo himself from preaching in public. And these persecutions, as more than one chronicler has remarked, came not from enemies of the Faith but from pious and able men zealous for the good estate and proper ordinance of Holy Church. The same phenomenon will be observable during the upheavals over the Discalced Carmelite reform in Spain three hundred years later. The angry Nuncio Cardinal Sega, who denounced St. Teresa as a restless, disobedient, and contumacious gadabout—"femina inquieta, andariega, desobediente y contumaz"[1]—and most of the Calced friars of Toledo who kidnapped and imprisoned St. John of the Cross were carrying out in the vigorous Latin manner what they conceived to be their

[1] August, 1578. St. Teresa, who had a strong sense of humour, echoes part of this diatribe in one of her letters.

duty by the Carmelite Rule. Good men strongly moved may act as hastily and unjustly as bad men. Human nature being what it is, this is nothing to be surprised about, though it seems so often to throw enemy observers into paroxysms of astonishment and indignation.

The immediate effect of Nicolas III's election on the Servite Order as a whole was naturally tonic and restorative. Anxieties ceased. The temptation to abandon a seemingly lost cause and join one of the major orders ceased likewise. Fra Filippo Benizi's tireless patience and energy during these trials entitle him to comparison with a naval captain holding his crew together in a disastrous engagement and bringing his ship out of it in triumph. He was well served by his officers, Fra Lottaringo, Fra Sosthenes, and Fra Ugo, and by what might be justly called, to vary a metaphor, the Old Guard of the Order, who had stood as firm under fire as Napoleon's *corps d'élite* at Waterloo. Having summoned the next chapter-general for June 1, 1278, at Borgo San Sepolchro, Fra Filippo was able to leave Rome with an easy mind.

Another notable recruit was to come into the order at Sansepolchro; a youth of great charm and personality named Andrea dei Dotti, belonging to one of the leading local families. He subsequently took Holy Orders, operated many conversions, and was beatified in 1806. ("One of our greatest saints", says the Servite chronicler Nicolas of Pistoia.) For the next few months there is little to record of Fra Filippo's movements. The order, now stabilised, continued to make headway and to expand. Fra Ristoro of Florence was appointed Vicar-General in France and Johann of Frankfort in Germany. Their prior-general's next undertaking will be of such import in the history of medieval Florence that one may despite oneself feel genuine surprise at Dante's omission to mention it. Dante was now, we may recall, fourteen years old, which is equivalent in general sophistication to the age of nineteen in terms of Anglo-Saxondom. One would have thought that the spectacle of his proudest and most bloody-minded fellow-citizens shamed into decency and surrendering at last to a humble Servite friar would have served him for a line or two in the *Inferno* at least.

It was indeed a considerable diplomatic feat, accomplished practically single-handed by Fra Filippo Benizi at the summons of a well-advised papal legate who turned to him without loss of time; "knowing", says the chronicler Tavanti, "in what esteem he was held by the citizens, both on account of his family and of his great prudence in the conduct of affairs, and even more so by reason of his saintly life". It was what nowadays would be called a triumph of personal relations.

2.

"I have known three-and-twenty leaders of revolts ..." In almost the voice of Browning's Legate Ogniben addressing the Provost of Faenza in *A Soul's Tragedy* the Cardinal-Legate Latino Malebranca might have ceased humming *Quare fremuere gentes* to assure the Podestà of Florence smilingly, had this been necessary, of his competence in the matter of handling public tumult.

He had already restored peace in the provinces lately restored to the Holy See by Rodolf I; in the Romagna, in Rimini and Cesena, Forli, Faenza, and Imola. He had even more skilfully brought the raging Lambertazzi and the furious Gieremei of Bologna to embrace each other publicly in the main piazza on August 4, 1279, and to swear on the Gospels to "live henceforth in peace and love". Cardinal Malebranca was undoubtedly aware on turning his mule's head towards Florence that he had the hardest nut of all still to crack. The patrician fighting-cocks of Florence were more numerous than elsewhere in Italy, more implacable, nursing deeper and older hatreds, more formidable rivals of Corsican or Spaniard in vin-dictiveness and pride. Fortunately the ideal Florentine was at hand to cope with them; their equal in rank, a public figure, a man of parts and eloquence, a recognised saint. The Cardinal-Legate's mule must have stopped outside the Annunziata priory very soon after he had paid his ceremonial call on the Signoria. As the new Protector of the Servite Order he knew Fra Filippo Benizi by more than reputation already. It is possible, though not certain, that Fra Filippo had been his coadjutor in the recent pacification of Bologna, having himself done a great deal there, as already observed, to restore the temporary peace of 1276. At all events there was no man in Florence better fitted to reason with his impossible fellow-citizens, who seemed at times to be more or less demonaically pos-sessed.

The City of the Flower had been in this state, as its historians set forth, for the last sixty years or more, ever since the assassination by the Amidei family of Buondel-monte dei Buondelmonti near the Ponte Vecchio on Easter Sunday morning, 1215. The young fop had grossly provoked the Amidei; a matter of dish-throwing at a banquet, jokes about a lady's face, a repudiated marriage-contract. To the Buondelmonti in the ensuing vendetta rallied the Adimari, the Pazzi, and the Frescobaldi—St. Philip's mother's people, as we may recall with legitimate interest. Twenty-five years later this quarrel, now embracing off and on a fair number of the citizens, blossomed into civil war with the passage of the Emperor Frederic II through Tuscany and the rise of the local Ghibelline faction, his supporters as all over Italy. By 1247 a running Guelf-Ghibelline conflict was occupying much of Florentine upper-class leisure. In 1248 Frederic's bastard son, Frederic of Antioch, marched into Tuscany with two thousand German troops and after hard fighting expelled the leading Guelfs and their families from Florence. The Guelfs took their vengeance after Frederic's death a couple of years later, returning from their rural fastnesses in force and driving out the disorganised Ghibellines from Florence in their turn. Ten years onward a large-scale pitched battle at Montaperti ended in a crushing Ghibelline victory, costing the Guelfs ten thousand dead, fifteen thousand prisoners, and a Ghibelline reoccupation. In 1267 the new King of Sicily, St. Louis IX's brother, Charles of Anjou—it would be excessively tedious to go into all the complications of this period—sent one of his captains, Guy de Montfort, with a strong French force to the assistance of the Florentine Guelfs, whose adversaries went into exile in the surrounding countryside of their own accord. Gregory X's unsuccessful attempt in 1273 to reconcile the irreconcilable has been already recorded. The Guelfs were undoubtedly to blame this time, and well deserved Gregory's interdict. They continued doggedly to reject every suggestion of peace, and the bloodshed and tumult continued in Florence and outside. Innocent V had meanwhile raised the interdict on the city in 1276.

By 1278, as if all the foregoing were not enough, a new folly had split the Florentine Guelfs, who were now divided among themselves, the Adimari fighting the

Donati, the Tosinghi, and the Pazzi. By this time an em-
bittered populace was liable to join at any time on one
side or the other. Such a lunatic imbroglio in due course
sobered even those responsible. Early in 1279 the leading
factions despatched envoys to Pope Nicolas III at Rome,
begging him to intervene; naturally in behalf of each.
Thus it came about that the Cardinal-Legate Latino
Malebranca, having pacified the Romagna and the city
of Bologna, rode at length into Florence and sought the
aid of one of its most outstanding citizens, the Servite
Prior-General, Fra Filippo Benizi.

Fra Filippo's labours, divided between exhortations
from the pulpit and continual conferences in private with
all the party-leaders, were entirely successful. Over and
above recognised sanctity and an eloquent tongue he had
the advantage, we may recall once more, of being the
social equal of his most arrogant fellow-citizens. The
ringleaders were the first to give in. Early in the new
year, 1280, the Adimari and the Tosinghi signified agreement to a reconciliation. The Donati, the Buondelmonti,
the Tosinghi, and the Uberti followed their example
within a few days. While Fra Filippo had been pursuing
private diplomacy Cardinal Malebranca had been at work
in the public sphere. Soon after his official reception by
the Signoria in October 1279 he laid the foundation-stone
of Santa Maria Novella. A little later he addressed the
municipality, the magistrature, and a vast concourse in
what is now the Piazza della Stazione, requesting the city
formally to grant him full powers. Accorded on the spot
with acclamation, these were confirmed on January 13. At
a meeting of the Council of Fourteen, or *Buoni Uomini*, at
the Signoria, the Municipality and Republic of Florence

put their city entirely at the Legate's service, under a
forfeit of fifty thousand silver marks. A week later,
speaking from a richly-hung platform in the centre of the
spacious piazza above-mentioned and surrounded by four
bishops and a large number of prelates and religious,
Cardinal Malebranca was able to announce to the populace
that the peace-terms were agreed. They were sufficiently
comprehensive. The form ran:

> Let there be concluded between the Guelfs and the
> Ghibellines a general, true, solid, and lasting peace. Let
> all lawsuits, quarrels, warfare, and enmities cease, and
> let the syndics of each party publish, in the name of
> both, a full and complete amnesty for all insults,
> offences, outrages, and misdeeds, and for all damage
> done. This shall not apply to real property or personal
> effects not actually destroyed. For these restitution
> must be made, even if they have been alienated by the
> City itself.

There followed the proviso that all outlawries and
other penalties, excepting those inflicted for private
offences, were cancelled, and that each party was to
appoint a hundred citizens willing to stand bail. Finally
it was proclaimed that the Ghibellines of Florence were
free to return and possess all their property and rights.

All being signed, sealed, and settled amid public rejoicing, the Guilds of Florence, taking their own time, as
was their wont, testified acceptance of the pact at a conference a week or two afterwards. It would be vain to
look for Messer Giacomo dei Benizi seated among the
dignitaries of his "Art", the Guild of the Apothecaries.
He was dead by 1276, to be unofficially and locally
beatified, with Donna Albaverde and their daughter Gio-

vanna, in due course. It was, as Fra Rossi explains, the routine of contemporary Italian hagiographers to assume that a saint's parents must themselves be saints.

Messer Giacomo would have been gratified by the warmth with which Cardinal Malebranca turned, before leaving for Rome, to congratulate and thank his humble coadjutor at the Annunziata, who had naturally kept in the background the whole time. The Legate's tributes to "this minister of the peace of Jesus Christ" and his public assurances that the healing of Florence was chiefly the work, under God, of Fra Filippo Benizi, Prior-General of the Servites, were reinforced by his proclamation of a forty days' indulgence, on the usual conditions, at the Santissima Annunziata on the Friday after the first Sunday in Lent. It may be noted in this connection that in the thirteenth century indulgences were granted far less often, and less amply, than they are to-day. The Legate's acknowledgment was followed by a considerable money-gift from the Republic of Florence towards the embellishment of the church and the enlargement of the priory of the Annunziata. There is a tendency among modern Florentine historians, noted Fr. Soulier in the 1880's, to diminish or even to ignore St. Philip Benizi's responsibility for Malebranca's success; an omission not exclusive to the anticlericals but noticeable even among "conscientious historians, members of religious orders, and Florentines proud of their city's illustrious sons". A handy illustration of this tendency is offered in the *Enciclopedia Italiana*'s long and erudite review of Florentine history down the centuries. Entire credit for the pacification of 1279 is given to Cardinal Latino Malebranca, and Fra Filippo Benizi is not mentioned at all.[1] Selectivity is, alas,

[1] Edition of 1932. Art. "Firenze".

an occupational disease among historians, and the *zèle du clocher* has been known to attack the holiest *scriptoria* when another order is concerned. There is no doubt of the extent and value of St. Philip's services to the Republic on this occasion. Many a minor Italian politician has been accorded a public statue impressive in size, however distressing aesthetically, for services far less noteworthy.

A more gratifying reward than anything the Republic could offer had come to Fra Filippo. Among the chief disturbers of Florentine peace was a member of the leading Guelf clan of the Adimari, a huge, quarrelsome swashbuckler of immense strength named Ubaldo, now in his late thirties. Brought up from childhood in an atmosphere of flaming pride and vengeance, twice exiled with his fellow-Guelfs, he had long since become a formidable duellist and a portent in Florentine affrays. Equipping him instinctively with an eagle beak and fierce hawklike eyes, one may very well see Messer Ubaldo degli Adimari stepping with his lackeys across a piazza in his steel hauberk and bassinet and particoloured hose, hand on sword-hilt, ready to spring as a tiger. He too was powerless against the arrow of grace. Accidental (as the world would say) contact with Fra Filippo Benizi during the late peace-negotiations changed Ubaldo's life. Not long afterwards, having made all possible reparation to his enemies, Ghibelline and other, he took the Servite habit and, after many penances and vigils, Holy Orders. A few months after his elevation to the priesthood Fra Filippo took Fra Ubaldo for his confessor, which speaks sufficiently for his new character, and he remained one of the best beloved of disciples until the General's death. After thirty-five years of the religious life Fra Ubaldo died in the odour of sanctity. His impressive remains rest in the chapel on Monte Senario, not far from the Founders' shrine.

3.

Not long after the pacification of Florence Fra Filippo received a letter from Rodolf I inviting him to Vienna. Having called a chapter-general on Monte Senario and, as twice before, invested Fra Lottaringo with the temporary government of the order, he proceeded to cross the Brenner, presumably accompanied as usual by Fra Vittore, and duly arrived at the Imperial Court.

A great deal had happened in the Empire since his previous visit. Its principal menace, Ottokar, King of Bohemia, had fallen on the field of Durnkrutt, where on August 26, 1278, some thirty thousand of his troops were routed after fierce fighting by an Imperial force a quarter their strength. As Rodolf I informed Pope Nicolas III, he regarded this, and his own escape from almost certain death in a hot mêlée, as a miracle. A less important adversary, Henry of Bavaria, could be dealt with at leisure. Against the turbulent heretics of Germany Rodolf had revived the decrees of Frederic II; that singular personage, himself intermittently excommunicate, was a great stamper-out of heresy. Those of the German nobility for whom the pillage of churches and monasteries had been almost a routine sport had been brought to heel likewise. Rodolf was a good friend to the religious orders and to the Servites especially, as a letter from Nicolas III ("... having so benignly welcomed our saintly Father Philip, showed him such affection, and granted his order so many favours ...") attests. The Czech chronicler Czerwenka

notes that during this stay Fra Filippo acted on several
occasions as the Emperor's confessor.

Visitations of the priories in the Empire, much preaching and several diplomatic missions, recalled by the
Emperor Leopold I in 1668, occupied him for several
months. A notable outlaw and assassin named Thomas,
taken singlehanded in a forest with his companions by
Frater Johann of Frankfort, was among the newest German recruits. He subsequently retired to Italy to live as
a hermit in the Appenines, returning to Cologne at his
superiors' orders to die a saintly death in 1288.

An urgent message from Fra Lottaringo cut Fra
Filippo's present visit short. With the death of Nicolas III
on August 22, 1280, the sky had suddenly darkened again
for the Servite Order. There was bad news concerning
Nicolas' successor, Martin IV, a Frenchman elected at
Viterbo in the following February. Like his late fellow-
countryman Innocent V he held the view, apparently,
that the decree of the Second Council of Lyons included
the Servites after all. Hastening back to Italy, Fra Filippo
summoned a chapter-general at Perugia. Here, on the advice of the venerable Fra Ugo, there present with brother-
Founder Fra Sosthenes, it was decided that the General,
with one or two chosen friars, should seek an audience
with the new Pope as soon as possible. They were duly
granted one on arrival at Orvieto. Once more Fra Filippo
put the case for the order, which need not be recapitu-
lated. Martin IV had apparently derived his impressions
of the situation from sources hostile to the Servites. He
listened and was enlightened. Without making any immediate decision he dismissed the General with kindness,
and with the understanding that no immediate danger
threatened his order. His opinion, after a first meeting, of

Fra Filippo Benizi himself is demonstrated by the fact that a few months later the Servite General was charged with an extremely difficult mission on behalf of the Holy See.

It was his old Florentine task over again, but magnified. This time the trouble-centre was the city of Forli in Romagna, a Ghibelline stronghold in open rebellion against the Holy See, its feudal lord. Commanding at Forli was the notorious condottiere-captain Guido da Montefeltro, to whom Dante devotes a whole canto of the *Inferno*, relating a story of Guido's later years which is one of the many conflict-points in the *Divine Comedy* over which commentators have raged and battled without issue. It involves Dante's abhorred Boniface VIII. At grips with the Colonna clan, he is alleged by the poet to have attempted to call Guido da Montefeltro out of retirement in his final penitent years as a Franciscan friar to lead the Papal troops against the Colonna citadel of Palestrina. Some modern scholars maintain that this story is mere hearsay embellished by the vindictive Dante. Others, naturally, oppose this view with equal verve.[1] In the year 1282, at any rate, Guido was still pursuing a military career and perjuring himself at intervals. In 1277 a strong body of troops from Bologna, Parma, Reggio, and Modena had tried to take Forli from him and had been routed ignominiously. In June 1281 a force of eighteen thousand men under the French captain Jean d'Epy, or d'Appia, despatched by Martin IV for the same purpose, was repulsed likewise and forced to fall back on Faenza, near which, some months later, it was cut to pieces. Intermittent appeals or demands by the Popes concerned had been rejected with insults. In May 1282, accordingly, Guido was excommunicated and the city of

[1] Masseron, *op. cit.*

Forli placed under an interdict. Having broken sworn pledges to the Holy See more than once, Guido can hardly be said to have been unfairly treated.

The citizens of Forli were, as may be imagined, in no mood to receive an envoy of the Holy Father with goodwill when Fra Filippo arrived in their city. Of glowering looks and insulting words and threats he took no notice, proceeding on entry to address an immense crowd in the chief piazza on their bounden duty. Jeers and ridicule from a band of youths developed swiftly into violence. Fra Filippo was beaten and driven out of Forli amid a shower of stones. Left bruised and bleeding outside the gates, he prayed for his assailants for some time and began then to take the Via Emilia in the direction of Cesena. At La Grotta, three miles out, according to a venerable tradition, he was overtaken by a youth of eighteen who had been the first to strike him in the face: one Pellegrino Laziosi, member of a leading local Ghibelline family. Remorse, forgiveness, penitence, conversion, and reception into the noviciate follow, the youth being identified as a forthcoming signal ornament of the order, St. Pellegrino. There would be no awkward dumb constraint or self-consciousness, or any shame at shedding tears. The youth would fling himself weeping and moaning in the dust at the feet of the elderly saint he had beaten; the saint would raise him up and embrace him, weeping with compassion and joy. A scene out of the *Fioretti*, it seems to-day, a grouping in blue and gold. It is curious to think that the same could once happen as naturally under a grey English sky.

A still more *Fioretti*-like scene attaches to the early summer of 1282. It follows the close of the chapter-

general at Viterbo, when the two holy and innocent old
men Sosthenes and Ugo, the last of the Seven Founders
but one, took their way back, climbing slowly hand in
hand to the priory on Monte Senario for the last time
and "holding", says Poccianti, "sweet converse together
on their road, like the two disciples on the road to
Emmaus".

Pausing from time to time to regain their breath and
to pray, they had nearly reached the top when they heard
a voice saying "Rejoice, men of God. Soon will your
prayers be answered." So, having returned home, they
began with serenity to prepare for a death which was not
long in coming. Only the liquid Italian of the old
chroniclers can render the final scenes worthily. The last
illness was very brief. Lying side by side on their hard
straw-covered pallets Sosthenes and Ugo received the
Viaticum and recited the prayers called the Crown of
Our Lady, and heard, as did all present, songs and speech
of more than mortal sweetness. " 'Come, Sosthenes', said
the Heavenly Ones, 'it is time to resign your spirit to
Him who gave it.' And taking that pure soul they carried
it before the Throne of the Lamb. Seeing which Blessed
Ugo exclaimed 'Wait, dearest brother! Pray wait for me!'
Even as he spoke his spirit took flight, and was borne to
Heaven with that of Blessed Sosthenes, to the joy of Our
Lady and the whole Court of the King."

Away in Florence that night St. Philip Benizi saw them
go in a dream. Says Poccianti:

He beheld two angels, who plucked two beautiful
lilies on the holy mountain and presented them to
Our Lady. And she received them with a glad count-
enance and offered them to her Son, who, placing them

in a jewelled vase, called to all the citizens of the Heavenly City, as they admired their spotless whiteness, to contemplate in them two perfect patterns of brotherly love.

On waking Fra Filippo called the community together to rejoice, for that "our venerable Fathers Ugo and Sosthenes, who with their five companions founded our order, have this last night fallen peacefully asleep in Our Lord. Now are they like two fair olive-trees and two burning lamps before the Throne. Let us therefore beg them to intercede for us and let us strive to imitate them, as far as in us lies, so that we may one day rejoice with them in everlasting life."

Thus six of the Seven Holy Founders of the Order of Servants of Mary were all together again. The survivor, St. Alexis Falconieri, was to live on, performing his lay-brother's duties, keeping accounts, begging alms, steadily resisting any suggestion of office, until 1310, having seen the order at last established by Papal authority and assisted his niece Giuliana to qualify for canonisation. Were any distinctions possible St. Alexis might be said, in his holy simplicity and love of obscurity, to express the Servite spirit more visibly than any of his brethren.

4.

We left Fra Filippo Benizi making his way, bruised and shaken, one day towards the end of 1282, along the road from Forli, whence he had been expelled with brutal violence, to Cesena. He did not return to Forli, the Ghibelline frenzy of the natives being irreducible. The year of the foundation of the priory there is supposed to be 1281. He made now for Arezzo, and was sufficiently recovered from his late experiences to be present shortly afterwards at the dedication of a new Servite church there.

We next find him presiding at the chapter-general of June, 1283, held at Siena. Otherwise there is no record of his activities for this year and the next, except that at about this time, according to traditional Florentine sources, he received St. Alexis Falconieri's niece Giuliana into the order as a *conversa*, or tertiary..As the foundress in due course of the Servite Third (Mantellate) Order, St. Giuliana has long been entitled to a niche in history and biographers of her own. She was at this moment fourteen years old, daughter of a noble and wealthy family and a nun by vocation, having rejected the suit of an eligible cousin and others of the young Florentine nobility and taken Fra Filippo for her spiritual adviser. Before long some of the smartest women in Florentine society were following Giuliana's lead and discarding the latest gowns for the black leather-girdled habit, scapular, veil, and cloak of the Mantellate tertiary; a procedure at which the magistrature of Florence, having issued a series of sumptuary edicts of which no well-dressed woman took the faintest notice, might well gape.

It is customary in Italy, as in every country in every age, to blame the French for the Florentine *haute couture* of the late thirteenth century and its elaborate immodesty. When Charles of Anjou, newly crowned King of Sicily by the will of the Holy See, descended on Tuscany in 1266 to dispossess Frederic II's son Manfred, he introduced a luxury and a laxity which its virtuous upper classes had never known before. Dante's great-great-grandfather Cacciaguida says as much to Dante in Paradise, extolling the good old days when "Florence within that ancient circle from which she still takes Terce and None [i.e., within those original ramparts from close to which rang the bells of the Badia] lived in peace, *sobria e pudica*, sober and chaste. No bracelets did she wear, no tiara, no embroidered gowns, no girdle taking the eye more than its wearer." A familiar lament down the ages from the dawn of time. "I saw Bellincion Berti walk girt with leather and bone", says Cacciaguida, in the very accents of Cato the Censor, "and his lady coming from her mirror with unpainted face".[1] Most of the fine ladies due to follow Giuliana Falconieri into the Servite Third Order painted their faces, plucked their eyebrows, exposed their bosoms, walked abroad in rich elaborate tissues decked with a profusion of jewels, and must have greatly resembled the fine ladies of any time. The morals of the smart took a downward trend simultaneously, by all accounts. Again it was the fault of Charles of Anjou. Apparently Boccaccio would have been at home in his native city a couple of centuries before his time. But the gambols of rich women are not a norm. Moreover, as we perceive, the smart set of late thirteenth-century Florence were not all blind or deaf to the eternal verities.

For a little time the new Mantellate nuns each lived at home, observing their own Rule, as the Servite and every other tertiary does to-day. When they had grown sufficiently numerous, St. Giuliana turned the Palazzo Grifoni, near the Annunziata, into a convent for those able to enter religion, herself continuing to live at home until her mother died in 1306, after which she joined and ruled them till her own death in 1341. By this time the Mantellate had many houses in Europe. Care of the sick was their especial charge. Some of the penances St. Giuliana

[1] *Paradiso*, xv.

inflicted on herself in expiation of her sins, such as they were, and those of others, and in conjunction with the Passion, make shuddersome reading for a Christendom grown soft; the Enemy recognised her worth and assailed her almost without remission for years. She seems also to have experienced, at her own supplication, something resembling that "transverberation" of agonising pain and joy which St. Teresa of Jesus experienced long after her, inspiring Bernini to the famous statuary-group in Santa Maria della Vittoria in Rome. She was canonised in 1737. Another outstanding recruit to the Servites round about this time was the saintly Sienese youth Francesco Patrizi, who took Holy Orders, became a notable preacher and confessor, and is venerated in Santa Maria dei Servi. From his grave before his translation, says a contemporary legend, sprang a lily, bearing the words "Ave Maria" in golden letters on its leaves, which was presented to Philip VI of France, a friend of the Servites of Siena.

In March 1285, just before Francesco Patrizi's reception into the order, Fra Filippo had a missive from the Papal Court at Perugia. Malebranca's urgent and momentous letter was an invigorating one. There were (wrote the Cardinal) excellent grounds for believing that definitive recognition by the Holy See was at last in sight. Pope Martin IV seemed to be in most favourable mood. With the aid of an advocate of eloquence, skilled in Canon Law, the long-wished-for final decision could almost undoubtedly be extracted from him.

Opposition to the existence of the Servites was in fact as vocal as ever in the Papal entourage, with tireless reference to the twenty-third decree of the Second Council of Lyons. Why hostility, open or veiled, should be so persistent might be explained in many ways, no doubt;

by misinformed good faith, or jealousy, or any other of what Dr. Johnson called the "anfractuosities" of human nature. Political misgivings were possible as well. The favours accorded the new order by such powerful secular princes as the Holy Roman Emperor and the Kings of France might well seem suspect to a certain type of Roman diplomat. Whatever the reasons, action was imperative. Scanning the order for a suitable advocate, Fra Filippo found one at the University of Paris, a Doctor of Theology and Canon Law named Henry. Sometimes confused with his namesake Henry of Ghent, known as "The Solemn Doctor", this learned friar proved eminently capable of what was required of him. At Perugia he opened the Servite case with forceful clarity. The main contentions we know. Having sufficiently developed these, Friar Henry argued that so far from inviting suppression the order had every reason to expect increased favours from Holy Church, given the Servites' international record so far. His peroration was a telling one. It was not, he said, so much his order which he was defending as its heavenly Patroness, to whom any attempt at persecuting her chosen servants was an insult.

The opposition's case being stated, Friar Henry refuted it in detail. Cardinal Malebranca then spoke in the order's behalf, followed by several of the consistorial lawyers who had examined the question in John XXI's time and judged in favour. When all had been heard Martin IV after due reflection gave judgment. In honour of the Mother of Sorrows, and in compensation for the trials and disappointments endured by the General, her servant, in recent years, the Holy See would confirm the Servite Order officially and extend its privileges.

A despatch from Malebranca conveying this happy

issue to Fr Filippo at Florence brought the General direct
to Perugia on muleback, save for a halt at Siena to receive
Francesco Patrizi. The mule, which cost the order the
equivalent of nine or ten pre-1914 English pounds, as Fra
Filippo's account-books show, was a luxury made
essential for the first time by reason of increasing age,
labours, fatigues, penances, and anxieties. On reaching
Perugia Fra Filippo was allowed by Heaven one crushing
disappointment more. He found the Holy Father stricken
with sudden illness and not expected to live. On April 28
Martin IV died, and with him, and for the fourth time,
all Fra Filippo's dearest hopes.

And yet again the sky cleared, almost immediately.
Four days later Cardinal Giacomo dei Savelli was nominated for the tiara, taking the name of Honorius IV.
Though his age, seventy-five, and his infirmities, which
compelled him to celebrate Mass seated, promised a reign
—actually one of three years—no longer than that of two
or three of his immediate predecessors, the new Pope was
known to be a good friend to the mendicant orders, and
had in addition a strong affection for the University of
Paris, his *alma mater* as it was Fra Filippo's. Cardinal Malebranca was swift to request an audience for the General.
Laying what were now routine-petitions at the Pope's
feet, Fra Filippo was kindly received and given good
reason to hope once more. When the aged Honorius left
later for Rome and coronation Malebranca saw to it in
Fra Filippo's behalf that among the papal train were men
of influence on the Servites' side. But growing trouble
with the French in Sicily was absorbing the Pope's attention, and no immediate decision was to be expected.

So Fra Filippo returned to Florence, to work and wait
in prayer and patience as before. After a chapter-general

on May 11 he called on the Signoria and asked the rulers
of the Republic to petition the Holy See vigorously in
behalf of an order native to their city. Given the Republic's recent obligations to him this was only reasonable. They assured him of willing co-operation. He then
began an intensive drive for alms, which the order
urgently needed. Recent legal expenses had been heavy,
and more were in prospect. The account-books of a saint
entangled with lawyers show a debit-side little different
from anyone else's. It was while he was thus engaged that
Fra Filippo was informed by an interior voice, one day or
night during prayer, that he had not very much longer
to live.

Thanksgivings for this good news offered, Fra Filippo
at once set about winding up affairs in hand with the
assistance of Fra Lottaringo, whom he had long since de-
signed as his successor. This concluded, he retired for a
space to the Monte Senario cave of former years to equip
his soul for the final journey. On Saturday, July 14, he
returned to Florence to announce to a chapter-general
called for that purpose that his time had come; and
having done so, knelt with them all and led the recital of
the *Nunc Dimittis*. "One of the old biographers", says Fra
Luigi Pazzaglia, "has endowed him with a long oration
on this occasion—too long, too elaborate, too classical,
too laboured to be his. We can be content with the cer-
tainty that he infused into his words all the sanctity of his
soul and all the paternal love of his heart." We know at
any rate that after addressing a stricken chapter on the
religious life and the precept of charity he knelt again and
prayed aloud for the good estate of the order, for all the
brethren, and for God's pardon on himself for faults and
negligences of his own. And as all present gave way to

their emotion again Fra Filippo dismissed them with his blessing and a cry of "Love one another, my dearest brethren, love one another, love one another." His life-long theme.

Next morning, with the chapter's unanimous vote, Fra Filippo appointed Fra Lottaringo della Stufa his vicar-general and next successor, transferring authority in the form appointed by himself and observed ever since; namely with the blessing of the Cross, the kiss of peace, and the handing over of the Book of the Constitutions. After an address from their ex-general on Our Lady's Sorrows, the inspiration of their order, on their vocation, and their duties, and a final blessing, the chapter rose, once more in tears.

No more remained to be done by Fra Filippo than to quit this life in peace. But he was determined to make one last journey to commend his order to the Supreme Pontiff's care. So, after a poignant leavetaking of the brethren at the Annunziata, he set out for Rome, accompanied by two of the religious, Fra Ottaviano and Fra Guido. Fra Filippo Benizi would never see the Annunziata or Florence itself any more. His parents were dead by 1275, and as already observed, due to be entered on the rolls of the Tuscan Province after his death as honorary *beati*, according to contemporary custom. His sister Giovanna, who became a Mantellate tertiary in 1284, was shortly to lose her husband, Forte da Sommaia, and to enter the Florentine house founded by her friend St. Giuliana.[1] Fra Filippo had no other ties with Florence outside the Annunziata. He had, moreover, decided already where to live his last days. The smallest and

[1] Rossi, *op. cit.* Donna Giovanna da Sommaia was similarly beatified after her death in 1300; also her son Forte, who entered the Servite Order in later years and achieved a reputation for sanctity.

poorest of all the Servite houses of Italy was the priory of San Marco at Todi in Umbria. Where could a General of the Servants of Mary, after a lifetime of evangelical poverty and humility, more fitly die?

On reaching the Papal Court, which was at Tivoli, Fra Filippo sought Cardinal Latino Malebranca and had a long talk with him, announcing the imminence of his end. At a subsequent audience with Honorius IV he did the same, begging a final blessing and imploring the Holy Father to protect the Servite Order and defend it against all who wished it ill. Affectionately reassuring him, the Pope dismissed him with a special benediction, and having embraced Malebranca for the last time, Fra Filippo, with his two friars in attendance, took the road to Umbria, sighting the red-tiled roofs of Todi in the late afternoon of August 9, 1285.

VI

SWAN-SONG

I.

TODI on its hill, ringed by Etruscan, Roman, and medieval walls, is a peaceful little city. In some of its narrow old streets one may catch even to-day a whisper of those "last enchantments of the Middle Ages" for which Matthew Arnold would have to listen very hard amid the racket of modern Oxford. Among its treasures are three Lombardo-Gothic communal palaces and half a dozen fine churches. In the crypt of San Fortunato lies Todi's most eminent son, the poet Jacopone, in whose achievement, as already remarked, the *Stabat Mater* is now included by all the most competent authorities—or rather, both *Stabats*, since Jacopone also wrote one on the Nativity, hardly known, making a perfect diptych.

> Stabat Mater speciosa
> Juxta foenum gaudiosa,
>   Dum jacebat parvulus;
> Cujus animam gaudentem,
> Laetabundam et ferventem,
>   Pertransivit jubilus ...[1]

[1] Denis McCarthy's translation:
> "By the Crib wherein reposing
> With his eyes in slumber closing
>   Lay serene her Infant-Boy,
> Stood the beauteous Mother, feeling
> Bliss that could not bear concealing,
>   So her heart o'erflowed with joy. . ."

Nothing seems more likely than that Fra Jacopone Benedetti of the Friars Minor was acquainted, if only distantly, with Fra Filippo Benizi. The combative lawyer-poet had become a friar at San Fortunato in 1278, a dozen years after Fra Filippo's foundation of the Servite house not far away. In such a tiny city as thirteenth-century Todi it is inconceivable that two such notable figures did not encounter each other. Had Fra Filippo continued to live a few years after his informal civic reception in August, 1285, the misadventures of Fra Jacopone—who may have taken part in it—would certainly have grieved him deeply. Might it be perhaps that the poet had only himself to blame, having sided with the formidable Colonnas against the no less formidable Boniface VIII, for being clapped into prison for five years, at the age of 68, by the commander of the Papal troops reducing Palestrina?[1] Fra Filippo would have instantly understood some of Jacopone's eccentricities before joining the Friars Minor, such as his reputed penitential crawl round the main piazza of Todi on all fours. It takes a certain effort to remind oneself nowadays that such self-disciplinary technique, like the public scourging of King Henry II after Becket's murder, is not necessarily covered by the routine-label "exhibitionism". What Fra Filippo made of some of Jacopone's satiric verse, if he ever heard of it, one may reasonably deduce. Its "bite", its Diogenes-like roughness, would have seemed to him a grievous sin against charity, which applies no doubt to all satire.

[1] Fra Jacopone had attached himself to a slightly fanatical Franciscan extremist group self-labelled "the Spirituals", living separate from community life by permission of Celestine V. Dissolved by Boniface VIII, the Spirituals were promptly backed by two cardinals of the Colonna family, his enemies. Jacopone was arrested at Palestrina, the Colonna stronghold near Rome, after its capture by papal troops in 1298; his satiric verse was chiefly responsible. Released 1303, died 1306.

We return to the summer of 1285, and the afternoon of August 9. There was a great bustle towards sunset in the streets of Todi. An exuberant populace was streaming down to the southern gate, carrying flowers and flourishing leafy branches. Before and among them went the magistrates and councillors and most of the clergy of Todi. Some horseman passing St. Philip and his brethren on the road had announced their approach, and a spontaneous mass-reception was afoot. But while the black-habited figures approaching Todi on foot were still some distance from the gates they were seen to stop, confer and turn in haste off the highroad, taking a bypath leading west to the river and emerging under the walls by the Orvieto gate, on the other side of Todi from the San Marco priory. Having perceived, to his dismay and horror, that the crowd ahead was already strewing the road with leaves and flowers, as if he had been some person worthy of honour, Fra Filippo hoped to escape round the walls and take refuge in San Marco undetected. As he and his companion-friars made their way round to the Orvieto gate two women stepped out of the shadows at a lonely part of the way and accosted them. These were prostitutes, it appeared; but, they sobbed as St. Philip questioned them with compassion, unwilling ones, driven to this shame by hunger and despair. One of the friars carried a little unexpended alms in the common purse, just enough for three days' bare subsistence. Handing it to the women, Fra Filippo implored them to leave off their trade for the next three days at least, and meanwhile to pray hard and commit themselves to God's pity and providence. Of their own accord they promised, weeping, to go to confession, and turned away. "What punishments, do you think, my brothers," asked Fra Filippo indignantly as the friars went on, "has Almighty God in store for those of the heartless and hypocritical rich who drive the poor into slavery like this?"

As he spoke they reached the Orvieto gate, to be met by a considerable crowd surging out with cries of "Ecco Filippo! Evviva il santo!" In a moment they were surrounded, and escape was impossible. Torn between affection and distress, Fra Filippo extricated himself for a moment from outstretched hands and signalled for silence. "O people beloved of God, my dear children of Todi, why do you come out thus to greet a poor sinner who is but dust and ashes? I am no saint! For the love of God give glory and praise to Him alone and depart to your homes in peace, allowing us to go quietly to our house, for we are very weary."

A nearby cleric in the crowd replied for the city at large.

"Father, we feel it our duty to honour you for your preachings, which have converted so many, and for your holiness, and the miracles you have wrought."

"In that matter, dear brother," Fra Filippo answered him mildly, "you err considerably. Beware of attributing the Creator's work to His creatures."

At length the excited crowd which was hemming them round, kissing Fra Filippo's hands and the sleeves and hem of his habit, consented to make way, and the three friars made their escape to San Marco. Entering the priory church forthwith to pray before the Blessed Sacrament, as was his wont at the immediate end of every journey, whatever his fatigue, Fra Filippo received an interior revelation of the date of his death. It was to be a fortnight hence, on Wednesday, August 22nd, the octave-day of the Assumption. Rising from his knees he

was heard by those around him to murmur *Gratias tibi
ago, Domine, quia haec requies mea in saeculum saeculi.*[1]

From now on the modest priory-parlour of San Marco
received a daily stream of visitors of all ranks and types,
from Angelario Bentivenga, Bishop of Todi, down to the
two penitent prostitutes encountered by Fra Filippo and
his companions near the Orvieto gate. According to Fra
Pietro da Todi, an eyewitness, these women came to San
Marco next day to make their confession to St. Philip in
person. Other chroniclers record their arrival three days
later, already shriven, to beg his advice concerning their
future. At their second visit Fra Filippo recommended
total withdrawal from the world and a life thenceforth of
intensive prayer and penance. The women, destined to
figure on the Servite rolls as Blessed Helena and Blessed
Flora, took him at his word. Having spent some months
of spiritual preparation in a cave on the slope of Monte
Arnolfa, about twelve miles from Todi, they entered a
neighbouring convent of enclosed Servite nuns, known
as the Second Order.[2] Meanwhile all Todi was flocking
to San Marco to hear Fra Filippo preach. There was to be
no rest for him and little opportunity for meditation. On
the Vigil of the Assumption, August 14, he prepared by
a rigid fast, using the discipline and refusing even a drink
of water in the heat of the day, for his last celebration on
earth of this great feast of the Universal Church, and of
the Servite Order especially. From daybreak on the feast
a great crowd began assembling at San Marco. After the
Gospel of a Mass said in an ecstasy of joy he ascended
the pulpit steps for what was to be the last time. His

[1] "Lord, I thank thee; for this is my rest for ever and for ever." (Psalm
cxxxi, 14.)
[2] An old tradition makes them the founders of the Second Order; but Rossi
is uncertain.

discourse, chiefly on the Beatitudes, ending in an invocation of the benediction of God and Our Lady on the city of Todi and all its inhabitants, has been described as a fitting swan-song.

At the hour of None, three o'clock that afternoon, Fra Filippo was seized with a disorder which rapidly developed into a high fever. Ordered to bed by the *infirmarius* he obeyed, yielding humbly to lawful authority as usual. Then exercising his own, he had the whole community called to his cell.

"Father Prior, and you, my beloved children, I have sent for you to tell you that the God of all goodness has been pleased, at the prayer of His blessed mother, no longer to delay in calling me hence to His rest."

He had only two favours to ask of them—firstly that his body should be buried without pomp or ceremony, like that of an ordinary lay brother, and secondly that they would continue to live after his death in fraternal love and reciprocal forbearance and charity. "Love one another!"—his theme-song was repeated this time with tremulous fervour.

"By God's grace I leave this order, of which I am the head, firmly established. Remember that if dissension should creep in, it will inevitably decay and fall to pieces, like a fortress with a divided garrison. But if there is concord among you, *carissimi*, this order, now deeply rooted, will grow and spread vigorously."

And again he returned to the theme of brotherly love. By now the whole community had broken down. Only the tender musical Italian of the old chroniclers once more can convey the passion of loving veneration shown by his friars for Fra Filippo at this news of farewell. They mourned their coming loss, says one contemporary account, with such vehemence of grief that for a space of nearly an hour afterwards there was not one of them capable of uttering a single word, *che per spatio quasi d'una hora no fu niono di loro che havessi forza di risponder una minima parola.*[1] Fra Filippo was able at length affectionately to rally and calm them. "Let infidels weep, and those who die in God's wrath! Surely to Christians, to whom Heaven is promised by the merits of our most holy Redeemer, the approach of death is rather a matter for rejoicing?" The Prior of San Marco with an effort replied, "in few words, but those of filial love", that their grief was but evoked by their devotion to their father in God. After vowing in their name to continue in the way of life their general had shown them he withdrew, with the others, and left Fra Filippo to his prayers.

These were interrupted some little time later by the entrance of the bishop, a Franciscan of sterling character who had always esteemed Fra Filippo highly. The sight of the Servite General lying consumed with fever on a plank covered with straw moved him to compunction. Apparently the doctor called in by the prior had already ordered a more comfortable bed and Fra Filippo, citing the Cross, had refused to give up his pallet. With the same humble and courteous obstinacy he disposed of all the bishop's urgings to the same effect; whereupon Bishop Bentivenga placed him forthwith under obedience and the matter was settled.

It was one thing to order a more comfortable bed in a poor Servite priory and another to find one. The community of San Marco all slept on planks and straw. They applied to a neighbour, one Messer Giacopo, a great friend of their house, and a woollen mattress was

[1] *Monumenta*, xiv.

immediately forthcoming. By this time Fra Filippo was in a burning fever day and night and in increasing pain, refusing nevertheless to have either his hair-shirt or his habit removed, choosing to die in armour like a soldier. His spirit was high and cheerful and he thanked God continually for allowing him to suffer with his Redeemer ("Lord, more suffering!"—one is reminded of St. Francis Xavier's dying cry on a desolate island off the coast of China some three centuries later). He continued in full exercise of his faculties, and, doubtless amid his doctor's despairing gestures, continued to receive a stream of visitors of all sorts seeking help, blessing, and advice.

On Tuesday, August 21, a great weakness came on him and he perceived that the end was near. Asking for a confessor, though he had received this sacrament more than once since his illness began, he again sought God's pardon for being an unprofitable servant, insisting on kneeling on the stone floor meanwhile. Afterwards he had the community called together and begged their forgiveness yet once more, in tears, for all his shortcomings in office. This anxiety disposed of, he requested the Viaticum in the morning and sank into meditation and a little sleep.

Early next morning the prior brought him the Blessed Sacrament from the church in procession, the whole community bearing lights and reciting psalms, and a number of laymen following. As the *Sanctissimum* was borne into his cell Fra Filippo rose from his mattress and knelt on the floor, addressing It, with passionate devotion, in almost the words of St. Thomas Aquinas now in the Missal. He ended:

And now, O uncreated Wisdom, I beseech Thee of Thine inexhaustible and infinite goodness, and through the merits of Thy blessed Mother, Mary ever virgin, to deign to watch over this new order, which is hers. Receive it, Lord, under Thy special protection, foster it with Thy tender care, protect it under the shadow of Thy wings, defend it from the cruel Enemy of mankind ...

And bequeathing his order, past, present, and to come, to God and Our Lady's protection, he came to the *Domine, non sum dignus*, received the Viaticum, and was gently laid down by the friars on his bed. After a pause he spoke to them again on heavenly things—"so wonderfully", says one of those present, "that we thought we were listening to an angel"—and returned again to mental prayer and meditation. Then after some time he bestirred himself and spoke faintly.

"My psalter."

They gave it to him, and he began to repeat the seven penitential psalms, very slowly, and the Litany of the Saints which follows them. When he came to *Peccatores, te rogamus*, etc.—"We sinners beseech Thee to hear us"—all present were shocked to see him turn livid suddenly and lose consciousness. For the next three hours he remained in a kind of stiff trance or coma, his features at times turning almost black, while the kneeling brethren prayed in anguish all round him. At length, assuming the end to have come, they left off in tears. As they gazed on him and each other burly Fra Ubaldo of Florence, the ex-swashbuckler, strode into the cell, covered with dust. At prayer on Monte Senario he had been inwardly warned of Fra Filippo's approaching end, and had forthwith covered the hundred-and-fifty miles to Todi on foot, under an August sun, in less than a week. As he embraced his apparently lifeless General, weeping and crying his name and shaking him gently, Fra Filippo came to himself at the sound of a well-loved voice and clasped Ubaldo in his arms. Collecting his faculties then he addressed the community round his bed. His voice was weak but clear.

"*Carissimi*, what a fight! The Enemy attacked me with incredible violence! To make me despair of salvation he paraded all my faults, assuring me that I deserve eternal punishment, and taunted me with them, and strove to drag me down with him to fire unquenchable. But Our Lord in His infinite mercy came at length to my aid, delivering me from that malignant Foe, and Our Blessed Lady stood by me also, turning aside and breaking the weapons of the Enemy. And when the prince of darkness had fled, They vouchsafed to show me the crown destined for those who have fought manfully; the incorruptible palm of victory; the throne prepared." [1]

It is a last trial permitted to and endured by many saints, a final privilege of the Elect, St. Thérèse of Lisieux being among the most notable in recent times. Reminding his friars that the invincible weapons against the Enemy all through life are abstinence, humility, patience, and charity, Fra Filippo asked for Extreme Unction, and was duly anointed. All was now ready for his departure, and with an expression of tranquil joy he composed himself to wait. But suddenly his hands fluttered over the bed. He was apparently trying to find something. He turned his head questingly from side to side with a worried look. They hung over him with questions. He spoke faintly and urgently.

"My book. Who has taken away my book? Find it for me, my dearest children."

They offered him his psalter. He shook his head. The

[1] Pietro da Todi, 1317; derived from St. Alexis and other intimates.

Gospels? No. Then the Office of Our Lady? No. Or the Rule? No, no, no. Finally Fra Ubaldo picked up at the bedside a little ivory crucifix which Fra Filippo had worn from childhood, and held it up inquiringly. Ah! Fra Filippo took and kissed it fervently. "My book", he murmured. "My book which has taught me everything. The Christian life! The way to Paradise! ..." He continued to contemplate the little crucifix, with frequent kisses, for nearly an hour. At length, as he was reciting the canticle from St. Luke's Gospel, *Benedictus Dominus Deus Israel*, the priory bell sounded the first three strokes of the evening Angelus. Fra Filippo's face lit up. He spoke again, clearly.

"Hark! The battle-trumpet of the Servant of Mary!" ("Ecco! La tromba guerriera del Servo di Maria!")

And he began Psalm XXX forthwith. "In thee, O Lord, have I hoped ..." At the last verse, *In manus tuas*— "Father, into Thy hands I commend my spirit"—some of those present were certain that they saw Our Lady in glory with the divine Child in her arms, surrounded by angels and welcoming her servant's happy soul. Before the Angelus-bell had stopped ringing Fra Filippo Benizi had departed. It was just after six o'clock of a serene August evening, the Octave of the Assumption, 1285. That night—to adapt the farewell words of St. John of the Cross, who three hundred years later left this earth at the first chime of his monastery-bells announcing Matins—Fra Filippo said Compline in Paradise.

Towards half-past eight the friars carried their General's body on a bier into the priory church, singing psalms of joy. The bells had been tolled. All Todi knew a saint was dead. The church and the adjoining streets were already thronged. Down the packed nave before long four men shoved their way, carrying a young twisted girl in a chair. She was a local notary's daughter, by name Agnavittina Guido, a paralytic almost from birth, carried there by her father's order. They lifted her up to kiss the folded hands of Fra Filippo as he lay before the high altar. On being set down on the pavement Agnavittina Guido rose, stood, and walked freely in the sight of all, cured and whole, amid a tempest of acclamations. After this it was impossible to dispel the crowds, and the church stayed open all night. Next morning, in the presence of the bishop and all the ecclesiastical and civic dignitaries of Todi, High Mass was sung in white vestments, with the introit *Gaudeamus omnes*, in place of the customary Mass of requiem; a substitution of joy for mourning approved by the bishop and entirely in accordance with Fra Filippo's own views on Christian leavetakings. In the course of this day seven more physical cures by contact with Fra Filippo's remains took place and were duly registered by four of the leading notaries of Todi at the bishop's order. The witnesses' depositions, with the names, addresses, and case-histories of the persons cured, are reproduced in the Servite Annals. One result of these happenings was that a bodyguard of friars had to be on duty day and night round Fra Filippo's open bier for the next six days. During this week the body, like that of so many other saints, showed no signs of deterioration in the heats of an Italian midsummer and a church thronged daily with citizens of every class, and exhaled that sweet fragrance which is the familiar atmosphere and token of sanctity.

On Tuesday, August 28, the saint's remains were removed to a tomb in the crypt, once more processionally and in the presence of all the notables of Todi and most

of the population. And the miracles continued. Twenty-
one cures by St. Philip's intercession were registered by
the end of 1285; there may even have been more,
unattested before the notaries owing to the shyness or
negligence of those concerned. They embrace cases of
paralysis, hernia, chronic rheumatism, tertian and other
fevers, ophthalmia, and demoniac possession. A child-
shepherd mangled by a wolf, picked up apparently dead
and restored to normal health at the saint's tomb, is
mentioned by Rucellai. Two vocal sceptics were taught
a lesson. Preaching at San Fortunato, one of the Friars
Minor to whom the church belonged was moved by
esprit de corps to rebuke the people of Todi for making
such an exhibition of themselves. His words as reported
are typical of the contemporary popular pulpit. "You
good folk must have lost your wits", he said. "One might
imagine Our Lord Himself had come down from
Heaven! Your credulity is quite absurd. Take my word
for it—it's all nonsense." Having uttered which he
staggered and fell, according to report, backwards in the
pulpit, and on recovery from a swoon found himself
unable to move or speak. His brother-friars carried him
forthwith to San Marco and prayed in his behalf at Fra
Filippo's tomb, and his rudeness was forgiven and his
speech and motion restored. The name of this friar is not
recorded. Among the community witnessing his dis-
comfiture and pardon was almost undoubtedly Fra
Jacopone da Todi, one of their elders. The other sceptic
was a local prostitute who remarked, possibly in a wine-
shop, as the bells of San Marco were tolling, "This
Brother Philip and his miracles—pooh! When all's said
and done he ate and drank just like any other fellow."
Temporary dumbness was this artless critic's lot as well;

her subsequent penitence ended in conversion and a changed life. How easy to wave away stories of this kind with a smirk! It is true that no one is compelled to accept them, yet how many printed stories less credible and comely are gulped unchallenged even to-day.

So we come to Operation Foray, briefly alluded to in an earlier page.

The citizens of Florence had received the news of the farewell celebrations and the miracles attending Fra Filippo's obsequies with an ill grace. An eminent fellow-citizen, a Florentine *de la vieille roche*, was seemingly being annexed and exploited by the inhabitants of a twopenny Umbrian burg of which nobody had ever heard. This could not be allowed. Whether or not pressure was brought to bear on the Annunziata is not clear. It would not have been abnormal for the Signoria to make representations to the General in their city's behalf. At any rate, Fra Lottaringo applied to Rome for permission for the body of Fra Filippo Benizi to be removed to his native city, and a brief from Honorius IV authorising this arrived in due course. Todi had other views. From the city councillors, or *Anziani*, and other leading burgesses, the Florentine emissaries learned soon that brief or no brief, the remains of Fra Filippo Benizi would stay in San Marco, where they belonged. The entire population of Todi belligerently concurred.

Between these clashing authorities the Prior of San Marco may be sympathised with. It seems obvious that his community, Todi men all, bore no responsibility in a *razzia* shortly afterwards. A well-organised midnight raiding-party from Florence was able to abstract Fra Filippo's coffin noiselessly from the crypt of San Marco, and had got away some little distance from Todi when the alarm was raised and a furious body of citizens sped in pursuit, returning triumphant with their recaptured treasure.

A second attempt of the kind some time later all but succeeded, the raiders decamping along the road to Perugia unpursued. On this occasion, according to the local story, the muleteer in charge of St. Philip's coffin lost touch with the main body and spent the rest of the night driving his pack-mule round and round a large stubble-field, at first believing himself to be on the road and at length, to his consternation, being unable to get out. At daybreak he was found at the gates of Todi, and surrendered. The saint's body was returned to San Marco once more and a shrine was erected on the field, with a commemorative inscription. Possible ocular testimony to this incident was still available in 1619, when a narrow circular track in the field concerned, faintly visible after the ploughings of more than three hundred years, was shown to the judges conducting St. Philip's canonisation process. As late as the 1880's Fr. Peregrine Soulier was informed by one of the canons of Todi that local farm-labourers were ready to testify that wheat sown on this track, now invisible, either did not grow or grew much shorter than the rest of the crop. Such evidence may not seem very convincing, and is not very valuable in any case; yet on the evidence of the same rustics, as Chesterton once pointed out in a similar English case, the law would hang a man. A belated last attempt to snatch St. Philip's body was made apparently on September 9, 1570. There are no details available. The alarm was given in time, as once before, and the Florentines gave up for good.

Meanwhile the saint's remains had been translated to a tomb more fitting. Fra Lottaringo raised the question at a chapter-general not long after Fra Filippo's death; but Fra Lottaringo was a Florentine, and Todi would have none of him. Under his next successor but one, the eighth general, Fra Pietro da Todi, it became a local concern. After a chapter-general in Siena in May, 1317, Fra Pietro, in the presence of the Bishop of Todi, removed Fra Filippo's remains on June 12, amid public rejoicings, to the chapel of St. Joseph in the priory church. Here they stayed, duly venerated, for the next two hundred and fifty years, with several more miracles of healing attributed to them. On August 16, 1579, the thirty-seventh Servite General, Fra Giacomo Tavanti, transferred them to a tomb under the high altar of San Marco. Twenty years later they were removed, for the third time, to Santa Maria delle Grazie, later renamed San Filippo, near the Porta Romana. This church had lately been given to the Servites in exchange for San Marco, handed over at the bishop's direction to the local Franciscan nuns, whose own convent was no longer habitable. Formally identified, and enclosed in a new cypress-wood sarcophagus covered with lead, while a familiar sweet fragrance once more filled the air, the body of St. Philip was conveyed processionally and chorally along the tapestry-hung streets, strewn with flowers, to Santa Maria amid the booming of cannon, the pealing of bells, the braying of trumpets, and the celebrations of a general festa.

To-day St. Philip Benizi's bones rest in a new tomb, recently constructed, of coloured marbles under the high altar of San Filippo. Enshrined in the high altar likewise is a reliquary presented in 1618 by the Massei family of Todi. It is a rectangular silver casket decorated with filigree and bearing on the front a miniature bust of St. Philip flanked by the arms of the Servite Order and the

Benizi; on the back are the arms of the Massei. Side-panes of crystal afford a view of the contents—a tunic known as the Cappa Santa, St. Philip's little ivory crucifix and rosary of the Dolours, and a red coral necklace believed to be one he wore in childhood. Two smaller reliquaries in the church and one in the sacristy contain a pair of his sandals, a pair of leather shoes given him by St. Clare of Montefalco, and half a white knitted cap. His cell is still shown in the former San Marco friary; his choir-stall in the church, covered, has not been occupied since his death. Rome, Florence, Perugia, and Budrio, twelve miles from Bologna, possess other Philippine relics; those treasured on Monte Senario and at Lucca vanished during the intermittent harassings of later and more liberal centuries. At Montefalco, twenty miles south of Perugia, the Augustinian nuns show a breviary, written on vellum and illuminated, given by St. Philip to St. Clare during a brief visit in exchange for the shoes above-mentioned.

In 1712 the local Office commemorating the final translation of the saint's body was extended by Clement XI to the whole Servite Order. It was only fitting that long before this his fellow-Florentine Pope Leo X, in the intervals of launching the Renaissance and grappling with its new heresies, should have officially sealed and extended a local cultus. Leo X did so in a bull dated January 24, 1516, raising the feast of Philip Benizi, thenceforth to be styled "Blessed", to the rank of a double, and authorising the Servite Order at large to announce it "by ringing their church bells and solemnising it by all customary ceremonies, all Constitutions of Alexander III and Innocent III to the contrary notwithstanding."

The way was now open to canonisation, for which there

was testimony already piled up of a whole sequence of miracles, past and present. Owing to the upheavals of Europe clients of this humblest of saints, himself so often disappointed, had to wait another century before his process was begun, and another fifty years before it was concluded. But his cause never lacked support in high quarters. In the early 1600's Ferdinand, Grand Duke of Tuscany, was only one of a group of Italian rulers urging the opening of Blessed Philip's process. In 1625 the reigning Holy Roman Emperor, Ferdinand II, addressed Urban VIII to the same effect. In 1641, in the thick of the Thirty Years' War, his successor Ferdinand III did the same, repeating his appeal to Innocent X in 1645. In 1668 the Emperor Leopold I wrote from Vienna to Clement IX:

> Your Holiness is not ignorant of the great services rendered during his lifetime—as the Acts of Canonisation further attest—by this zealous Servant of Our Lord in spiritual matters, especially in cases of conscience; of the abundant nourishment for souls derivable from the pious practice, introduced by him, of wearing the Scapular of Our Lady of the Seven Dolours, the scapular with which he invested Our predecessor, the Emperor Rodolf I of glorious memory; of his success in many difficult negotiations entrusted to him by the same Emperor; and lastly, of his marvellous piety and sanctity, whereby his light shone before men, and of the glory which God gave him during his life and has continued to give him since his death, as testified by innumerable miracles ...

Reminding the Holy Father of the letters addressed to his predecessor in Blessed Philip's behalf by Ferdinand III and the Empress Maria, "our most honoured mother of happy memory", the Emperor proceeds:

Treading therefore in the steps of Our august parents, We, with that filial respect and absolute submission We ever tender to Your Holiness, earnestly beseech You, after having completed the usual formalities, to enrol the said Blessed Philip in the ranks of the saints. For We proclaim Ourselves bound to this holy Servite Order by strong ties of gratitude, having experienced in Our childhood, in a marked and miraculous manner, the efficacy of the Scapular of the Seven Dolours. This favour, which We ask with all earnestness, We look for with confidence from Your Holiness. And We now pray that the divine goodness may preserve Your Holiness for many years, and for the greater good of Holy Church.

Given in Our city of Vienna, on the twenty-fourth of December one thousand six hundred and sixty-eight, the eleventh year of Our reign as King of Rome, the fourteenth thereof as King of Hungary, and the thirteenth as King of Bohemia;

Your Holiness' respectful Son,
LEOPOLD.

He wrote to the same effect to Clement IX's successor, two years later, as did the Grand Duke of Tuscany and members and friends of the Servite Order all over Europe. At length the Holy See responded. On the second Sunday after Easter, April 12, 1671, Blessed Philip Benizi was raised by Clement X to the altars of the Universal Church with four other new saints: St. Francisco Borgia, ex-Duke of Gandia and third General of the Society of Jesus, St. Gaetano Cajetan, founder of the Theatines, St.

Louis Bertrand, O.P., apostle of New Granada, and St. Rose of Lima, that rose, to quote the fragrant office of her feast, which, "watered by the heavenly grace, blossomed in the Indies as a lovely flower of virginity and patience". All Rome was illuminated. In Florence there was a great firing of cannon and pealing of bells, with a procession of the Signoria and the Guilds, and fireworks on the Annunziata piazza and elsewhere for three consecutive nights. At Todi similarly. In 1599 Fra Filippo had been formally proclaimed "Protector and Defender" of the little city. Many others in Italy followed suit.

Nearly three centuries earlier the Order of the Servants of Mary had, as already noted, been officially recognised at last and confirmed in all its constitutions and privileges by the bull *Dum levamus* of Benedict XI, dated February 11, 1304, under the generalship of Fra Lottaringo's immediate successor Fra Andrea Balducci, seventh of his line. The feast of St. Philip Benizi, with its proper rank, was extended to the whole Church by Innocent XII in 1691.

EPILOGUE

"THAT love which moves the sun and the other stars", *l'amor che move il sole e l'altre stelle*—the last line of the *Paradiso* expresses the essence of St. Philip Benizi's message for the Atomic Age, as for any other: love, humility, patience, compassion, self-sacrifice, self-effacement, the sharing of the sufferings of the Mother of Sorrows with the seven swords in her heart—the only one of all human creatures, as Huysmans remarks, over whom, logically speaking, since she was sinless, pain had no rightful power. "It needed God's special permission and the consent of the Mother, who, to make herself more like her Son and to co-operate, according to her capacity, in our redemption, accepted at length, under the Cross itself, the frightful agonies of the Consummation."[1] It was St. Philip's work, as it is that of all of his order, to make this colossal mystery of pain intelligible to the simplest mind. He succeeded with emperors as with woodcutters. To an age of scientific devilries which make the thirteenth century look like a kindergarten he speaks with added force.

Though Fra Alessio Maria Rossi, in his recent history of the order, could hardly omit listing the many Servites who have distinguished themselves since the thirteenth century in letters, arts, sciences, and public service, its *raison d'être* remains evangelical, as the Seven Holy

[1] *L'Oblat*, 1903.

Founders made it. Fra Rossi himself defines the Servite ideal as the effort to attain Christian perfection by the practice—by religious, tertiaries, and the mass of the faithful alike, according to their several means—of the three great evangelical counsels, in dedication to Mary and in her service. The essential of this religious life, adds Fra Rossi, coining "an impossible word", is to be *marianizzato*, or Marianised; to enter into close contact with Our Lady, to have one's whole spiritual being permeated by her holy example, to regard her not as a saint but as *the* Saint. As the Jesuit poet sings:

> Mary Immaculate
> Merely a woman, yet
> Whose presence, power is
> Great as no goddess's
> Was deemed, dreamed; who
> This one work has to do—
> Let all God's glory through,
> God's glory which would go
> Through her and from her flow
> Off, and no way but so ...[1]

Testimony to Our Lady's response down the ages is not lacking. Not the least notable of the Servite feats in modern times was performed under a century ago, when the Frati Agostino Morini and Filippo Bosio arrived, penniless, speaking little or no English, from Florence and Rome respectively and founded the order's first English parish in the ultra-Protestant and xenophobe London of the 1860's. The two friars, both learned in theology and canon law, had that pre-eminently Benizian blend of

[1] Gerard Manley Hopkins, "The Blessed Virgin Compared to the Air We Breathe."

serene simplicity and holy obstinacy which foils the world. Walking the grey streets of London in the top hats and frock coats, barely disguising their identity, which were the only safe clerical garb of that place and time, they differ no otherwise from St. Philip's black-habited companions under a thirteenth-century sky. In a strange and hostile land, moreover, they were receiving gloomy news from Italy; the religious orders were being harried by the liberals of the Risorgimento and Monte Senario itself was in danger. "Lucky the man who has the good fortune to be in England now", said one wry letter from Florence—*beato chi si trova in Inghilterra*.[1] Our Lady brought them through everywhere. In Italy the clouds dispersed. In London a fine large Servite church and priory had risen by 1875, and other foundations in Great Britain were being planned. The Servite mode of operation was the same as it had been from the beginning; poverty and humility and strong faith triumphing over every obstacle.

In that great series of frescoes by Luca Signorelli in the Capella Nuova of Orvieto Cathedral which so happily survived World War II is a famous figure of Antichrist enthroned; a noble and handsome and impressive personage until you get close and see the sneer. In Signorelli's time he lacked the tremendous publicity-weapons of which Pope Pius XII spoke in his "Apostolic Exhortation" to the world's priesthood on Passion Sunday, 1949:

> With supreme insolence the enemies of the Name of God avail themselves of every kind of help and advantage. Books, periodicals, the Press, the radio, organisations, public meetings, private interviews,

[1] Gerard M. Corr, O.S.M., *op. cit.*

education, culture—all are at their service to spread
ridicule of sacred things. "The smoke of the pit arose,
as the smoke of a great furnace, and the sun and the air
were darkened with the smoke of the pit." We consider, venerable brethren, that this does not take place
without the insidious machinations of that infernal
enemy whose nature it is to hate God and to injure man.

So the battle continues, increasingly fierce, and there
may be moments when faint hearts in despondency need
to recall divine assurances and Marshal Foch's historic
communiqué halfway through the Battle of the Marne,
in which a great Catholic soldier speaks for a greater
conflict still: "My right is giving way. My left is retreat-
ing. Situation excellent. I attack." Antichrist is by no
means enjoying a triumphal progress, as he occasionally
admits with some heat. The forces opposing his own are
war-wise and formidable—"How many divisions has the
Pope?" asked Stalin satirically, revealing the essential
rustic—with resources timeless and beyond his ken and
a cause indestructible.

Among the *corps d'élite* of God the religious orders keep
up the counter-attack with inexhaustible vigour and every
kind of spiritual weapon, beginning with the Holy
Rosary. Each has its position in the front line, and no
comparisons are possible. But we may reflect that the
black-habited division raised seven hundred years ago by
seven citizens of Florence and commanded for fourteen
memorable years by St. Philip Benizi can show as considerable battle-honours as any.

It is a convention of modern biographers, having summoned up some notable figure of a bygone age, to conclude by waving him an elaborate farewell as he recedes

again into the mists of the centuries. St. Philip does not recede at all. One has no need to travel to his native city to encounter a frail, calm, vital figure, very much alive, surrounded by light, still dispensing the good news of Christ in a sweet fragrance of sanctity. Far removed from us in time and space, his presence and inspiration can be vividly felt in every Servite church in the world, however uninspired the efforts of Repository Art—which is saying something—to recall him physically, however feeble the glimmer of such a brief candle as these pages attempt to offer him. To have at call two great fellow-citizens active in Paradise, each named Philip, one of the Middle Ages and the other of the Renaissance—how fortunate is the City of the Flower, how fortunate are we all.

THE END